Seminary Theology III
Seminary Formation and Psychology

Edited by Deacon James Keating, PhD

D1452855

The Institute for Priestly Formation
IPF Publications

CONTRIBUTORS

Suzanne M. Baars, MA, PhD (cand.), LPC, LMFT, is a licensed professional counselor and marriage and family therapist in Irving, Texas.

Kathryn M. Benes, PhD, is Director of Regina Caeli Clinical Services in Denver, Colorado.

Antony Bond, PsyD, is affiliated with St. John Vianney Theological Seminary and Regina Caeli Clinical Services and is currently completing his post-doctoral residency in clinical psychology in Denver, Colorado.

Edward Hogan, PhD, is Director of the Pontifical Paul VI Institute of Catechetical and Pastoral Studies and an Associate Professor at Kenrick-Glennon Seminary in St. Louis, Missouri.

Christina P. Lynch, PsyD, is Director of Psychological Services for St. John Vianney Theological Seminary in Denver, Colorado.

Father Walter Oxley, STD, is Vice-Rector for the School of Theology at the Pontifical College Josephinum in Columbus, Ohio.

Christopher J. Stravitsch, MA, LPC, LMFT, has served on the Formation Faculty of Assumption Seminary and is also the Executive Director of Rejoice Family Apostolate and Founding Vice President of The John Paul II Foundation for Life and Family in San Antonio, Texas.

NIHIL OBSTAT: Father Matthew J. Gutowski

IMPRIMATUR: Most Reverend George J. Lucas
Archbishop of Omaha, Nebraska
September 12, 2013

THE INSTITUTE FOR PRIESTLY FORMATION, INC.
IPF Publications
2500 California Plaza
Omaha, Nebraska 68178
www.IPFPublications.com

Printed in the United States of America
ISBN-13: 978-0-9887613-1-5

Cover design by Timothy D. Boatright
Marketing Associates, USA
Tampa, Florida

THE INSTITUTE FOR PRIESTLY FORMATION
MISSION STATEMENT

The Institute for Priestly Formation was founded to assist bishops in the spiritual formation of diocesan seminarians and priests in the Roman Catholic Church. The Institute responds to the need to foster spiritual formation as the integrating and governing principle of all aspects for priestly formation. Inspired by the biblical-evangelical spirituality of Ignatius Loyola, this spiritual formation has as its goal the cultivation of a deep interior communion with Christ; from such communion, the priest shares in Christ's own pastoral charity. In carrying out its mission, the Institute directly serves diocesan seminarians and priests as well as those who are responsible for diocesan priestly formation.

THE INSTITUTE FOR PRIESTLY FORMATION
Creighton University
2500 California Plaza
Omaha, Nebraska 68178
www.priestlyformation.org
ipf@creighton.edu

TABLE OF CONTENTS

INTRODUCTION

DEACON JAMES KEATING

Affective maturity presupposes an awareness that love has a central role in human life. In fact . . . "Man cannot live without love. He remains a being that is incomprehensible for himself; his life is meaningless, if love is not revealed to him, if he does not encounter love, if he does not experience it and make it his own, if he does not participate intimately in it."

We are speaking of a love that involves the entire person, in all his or her aspects—physical, psychic and spiritual . . . . (Blessed John Paul II, *Pastores Dabo Vobis*, sec. 43-44)[1]

This volume is the result of our annual Theological Seminar held on the campus of Creighton University and sponsored by The Institute for Priestly Formation. During the course of the seminar, the participants were asked to reflect upon the role that psychological science plays in helping the Church bring forth men of affective maturity within the priesthood. The psychological sciences, when based upon a legitimate Christian anthropology, assist seminary formators in their work of leading seminarians to the true freedom of spousal self donation. As Blessed John Paul II notes above from his Apostolic Exhortation *Pastores Dabo Vobis*, a man must be able to gift the Church with a love that encompasses his "entire person." Throughout the essays in this volume, which is aimed to assist all those who labor in the area of human formation within the Catholic seminary culture, the reader will find that one of the prerequisites for such love is mental and affective health. Such health facilitates the free response of a man in saying, "Yes" to God's call to priesthood. For without emotional and psychic freedom, no true gift of self can be bestowed. Further psychology can assist in a man's "recovery" from the contemporary popular and political culture which has already formed some men in deep ways of thinking and feeling that may be antithetical to a vocation.

It is the hope of the seminar participants that their contributions will aid the Church in thinking more specifically about the nature of affective maturity within the context of priestly formation. Psychological health, moral freedom, and spiritual desire conspire to give the Church what it needs in its priests: men who freely and eagerly donate their bodies, their entire selves, so that Christ can live His priesthood over again in them.

NOTES

1.   Also see the promotion of psychology in the work of ongoing formation of priests, as well, in Congregation for the Clergy, *Directory for the Ministry and Life of Priests* (new ed.) 2013. sec. 93

THE ROLE OF AFFECTIVITY IN FORMING THE MAN OF COMMUNION: RECEIVING THE PRIESTLY IDENTITIES

SUZANNE M. BAARS

The formation of a man for the priesthood and assisting him toward becoming a man of communion is rooted in affectivity, the capacity to be moved by the goodness of another person. Blessed John Paul II said that "man has been made in the image and likeness of God not only by his being human, but also by the communion of the persons that man and woman have formed since the beginning. They become the image of God, not so much in their aloneness as in their communion."[1] Deacon James Keating notes, "The Church envisions human formation to be a set of relationships that enable a seminarian to become a man of communion."[2] The candidate for priesthood should be a man of communion, so "that he becomes someone who makes a gift of himself and is able to receive the gift of others."[3] A man must *receive* the priestly identity from God Who endows each human being with a mission. However, becoming a man of communion is not accomplished solely on the spiritual level. As such, every dimension of the man–physical, spiritual, intellectual, and emotional–must be considered.

The priestly identities of spiritual father, spiritual physician, and good shepherd hinge on those first received: beloved son and chaste spouse.[4] Just as the child moves through developmental and relational stages of son or daughter to sibling to spouse and only then to parent, so, too, the identity of the priest must be rooted in that of sonship, from which he is readied to become spouse, and once spouse, he can become father. Moreover, without the human relationships from which he derived affective integration, a man is not capable of a full and free gift of self. In fact, this self-donation will certainly be hampered by any deprivation of affirmation a man has experienced in his early relationships, around which his life will then be focused.

The priestly identities of beloved son and chaste spouse are foundational to those of spiritual father, spiritual physician, and good shepherd. Therefore, it is important to discuss the psychological needs of the human person foundational to the formation of an integrated personality.

Relationship: The Source of Identity

The human person is made for relationship. As man is the image of God, and God is a Communion of Persons, so, too, man is made for relationship, to live in a communion of persons. The fact that we are made for relationship with God and in Him we find ourselves is not simply a spiritual or intellectual truth, but it is, in the order of nature, a psychological truth. In Genesis, God said, "It is not good for the man to be alone" (Gn 2:18). Adam was not told by God that

all would be well, that He alone was enough; God created a
new person, Eve, to be with Adam. God creating Eve con-
firms that, in a very real sense, we need others. Furthermore,
it is primarily our relationships with our parents or other
significant caretakers which first form our identity and our
sense of ourselves as good, worthwhile, and lovable. Indeed,
these relationships can strengthen or weaken us and, thereby,
directly affect our capacity to love. Every relationship will be
stamped with either the person's confident self-possession,
or with the absence of self-confidence and the drive to fill
whatever needs have not been met.

His Holiness Benedict XVI has said, "...human beings
were created in the image and likeness of God for love, and
that complete human fulfillment only comes about when
we make a sincere gift of ourselves to others. The family is
the privileged setting where every person learns to give and
receive love."[5]

It is pertinent in a discussion of seminary formation to
address how persons come to be affectively mature, thereby
possessing the capacity for relationship and the mature
freedom for commitment, either in marriage, priesthood, or
religious life. Ideally, a child's first relationships in life should
have provided him with emotional strengthening, through the
receptive presence of his mother and father. This strengthening does not occur in some idealistic or spiritualized way, but
rather, in a specific, tangible way, through the loving openness
of his parents. This attitude of affirming presence by one's
parents is the first house of formation which shapes the heart
of the future priest. Jesus, Himself, experienced this affirming
presence in His relationship with Mary and Joseph at Nazareth; indeed, the fact that He created the family and deigned

to live in one Himself emphasizes the importance of the communion of the family in God's plan for human development and happiness.

It is in this community of the family that one first may experience an authentic communion of persons, if the family is oriented towards the good of each of its members. His Holiness Benedict XVI notes:

> Father and mother have said a complete "yes" in the sight of God, which constitutes the basis of the sacrament which joins them together. Likewise, for the inner relationship of the family to be complete, they also need to say a "yes" of acceptance to the children whom they have given birth to or adopted, and each of which has his or her own personality and character. In this way, children will grow up in a climate of acceptance and love, and upon reaching sufficient maturity, will then want to say "yes" in turn to those who gave them life.[6]

He adds, "The family is also a school which enables men and women to grow to the full measure of their humanity. The experience of being loved by their parents helps children to become aware of their dignity as children."[7]

Through familial relationships which foster growth and freedom in a loving atmosphere, mind, heart, and body can be integrated naturally over time. This process permits the affective heart to develop at the center of a life lived open to others, while the effective mind can then be oriented to the good recognized by the heart.

Affectivity and Effectivity

The importance of this development of the affective,

intuitive heart before that of the working mind is borne out by the late Catholic psychiatrist Conrad Baars: "[R]eason and will are not the only principles of the human act. The emotions are positive principles which add moral value to the human act. Having a feeling, a liking for the good, definitely adds something to the moral value of the will-act. It is not only psychologically important to strive after the good with heart and soul, but also morally better."[8] Baars notes that Aquinas taught that the will is not meant to be the sole principle of human acts. In fact, the will not only moves, but is itself moved. "The will must first be moved *affectively*...[as in being] 'moved to tears'. If at all possible, the good must please the will emotionally, and at the same time appeal to it via reason. To will, in the broader Thomistic concept, is first of all *affectivity*. Only secondarily, and dependent on this affectivity, is the will an active mover–*effective*. Virtue, therefore, is not only in the will and reason, but also in the emotions."[9]

Baars defines these terms more specifically: affectivity is "the habitual disposition of the heart to be moved by the good of the other (and other things and beings) and to act on his behalf. Affectivity consists of the fully or adequately developed emotions of the [concupiscible] appetite in their close interaction with the intuitive intellect. ... Effectivity (is) the habitual disposition of the mind to see and grasp the other (and other things and beings) for his own utilitarian purposes..."[10] While effectivity is necessary for human life inasmuch as it assists one in the accomplishment of tasks, developing one's affectivity is absolutely necessary if a man is to experience the happiness for which he is created.

The complementarity of affectivity and effectivity is a necessary element in human development. Moreover, effectivity must be predicated upon affectivity, just as *doing* follows *being*. When the relationship of these two aspects of human life is reversed, the person's focus in life becomes utilitarian, and his relationships necessarily suffer. Nurturing and guarding one's affectivity is crucial to preventing it from being smothered or destroyed by the attitude of unmitigated effectivity present in our utilitarian, materialistic world.

Affectivity in Relationships

Authentic, affirming love, rooted in affectivity, provides an encounter with the self through another who allows himself to be moved by the goodness of the person. In the first community of the family, it is in seeing our parents moved by our own goodness that informs us of our own unconditional lovability. It is important to note that authentic affirmation is not a matter of *telling* the person the truth about himself, nor is it a type of technique designed to build self-esteem. Rather, living in an affirming way is a process whereby one is willing to be open and receptive to another; second, he permits himself to be moved affectively by the unique goodness of the other (as he gradually comes to know the person), and third, he *reveals* his feelings about the other in his countenance, tone of voice, choice of words, etc.[11] This affirming encounter takes place on the level of the heart rather than on the level of the intellect. Such a form of communion reveals to him his unique goodness as a person, thereby strengthening him to be *himself*.

Much is discovered about another when one is still and silent in his presence. It is in this attentive stillness that one's mind is quiet and receptive, and one encounters the other on the level of the heart. This stillness, this quiet attentiveness, is simply open and receptive rather than expectant. It is affective rather than effective. This crucial distinction between affectivity and effectivity provides the possibility of heartfelt *communion* rather than mere *communication.*

In terms of a person's primary, formative relationships, one might say that the mother's love is the first gaze which draws the boy into a mutual relationship of love. Having experienced the invitation to love and be loved, he is equipped to give away what he has received: he knows the value of merely being present to others. When he is older, it will be the father's love which calls him into a new kind of relationship, one which affirms his place in the masculine world and strengthens him to be courageous as well as gentle in teaching, preaching, and evangelizing.

To the contrary, the child who has been left to himself by his parents in order to "toughen him up" and make him independent, ironically, becomes *less* capable of being independent, as he is deprived of the innate need to be loved unconditionally, which by necessity, becomes the focus of his life as he grows into adulthood. His heart will be restless, seeking what it has not received in the order of nature. This lack is not ordinarily overcome by the order of grace, as God has ordained that the human person mature over time within the context of human relationships. The man who becomes a priest in this affectively un-integrated state will lack sufficient capacity needed to *love* his Bride, the Church, as spouse, father, physician, and shepherd. *Affective maturity* is achieved only on the intuitive level of the heart, where one naturally needs to receive love before one can give love. Similarly, intellectual maturity can be achieved only on the intellectual level, where one naturally must receive the truth.

To expect that affective maturity comes through spirituality or solely through intellectual discourse or spiritual direction is not reasonable. Therefore, in assessing candidates for priesthood, examination of the early relationships of the candidate is critical. Of course, in an era where the disintegration of the family is commonplace, rectors and formators can be helpful to seminarians by recognizing the needs of these men and by providing an authentically affirming environment within the seminary itself, in which affectivity is nurtured. This affirmation may be sufficient to assist the growth of all but the most severely emotionally deprived men.

From the emotional strengthening as son in his familial relationships, the man is able to turn toward others. In having been "received" by his parents, he has been given the gift of himself; and because of this gift, he knows also how to give. He is ready to become a spouse.

> Betrothed love comprises on the one hand the gift of the person, and on the other hand, acceptance of that gift. Implicit in all this is the "mystery" of reciprocity: acceptance must also be giving, and giving receiving. Love is of its nature reciprocal: *he who knows how to receive knows also how to give....*a man is capable of fully accepting a woman's gift of herself only if he is fully conscious of the magnitude of the gift–which he cannot be unless he affirms the value of her person. Realization of the value of the gift awakens the need to show gratitude and to reciprocate in ways which would match its value.[12]

Now the man is ready to be spouse–open to receive the goodness and lovableness of the spouse into his heart, and to reflect this *felt* sense of her goodness to her. This openness forms the *bond* which is the "vehicle" of the relationships over the course of his life, transporting him, so to speak, toward deeper acts of love, service, and self-sacrifice for his beloved–the greatest being the capacity and willingness to restrain his own desires for the sake of the other. Having been loved unconditionally, the man is no longer alone, locked as a prisoner within himself; and so his receptivity and affectivity may now blossom and will have the power to be generative. Whether the man actually becomes generative naturally depends entirely upon his freedom to accept or reject the Divine call to love others, whether he responds to this call by remaining open and receptive himself, and whether he guards his affectivity.

It is, moreover, important to note that the man's capacity to experience a *felt* sense of his own goodness is the basis for being able to experience a *felt* sense of the goodness of the spouse. Whether in marriage or in chaste celibacy as priest, the man's capacity to be moved affectively by the goodness and beauty of others has a direct bearing not only on his own capacity for happiness, but also on that of his spouse, the Church. The Church's experience of her spouse, the priest, will in certain ways parallel the woman's experience of her husband as a loving, caring, and protective spouse.

The order of grace builds on this natural encounter. In his encounter with God in his prayerful imagination, the priest experiences the affirming gaze of the Father, who reveals to him, "You are my beloved son!" This is not merely a truth *told* to the priest in order that the priest understand and execute his mission; this truth is communicated and received *affectively*, meaning that the heart of the priest is moved–and in being loved, the man/priest *experiences* his worth as beloved son. Having already received his identity, he has no need to search for it in others or material things; he has been equipped to move out of himself toward others. Having been strengthened by receiving the gift of himself, which can only come through the affirming presence of another person, the man becomes truly capable of authentic love. The fact that he is a "conscious, free and responsible person,"[13] however, denotes that he is still free to refuse to love. Yet, this profound freedom comes from the affective integration arising through authentically affirming relationships. Although capable of enjoying solitude, he is no longer alone; he knows the experience of mutual, unselfish love. It is without doubt that one's identity, one's sense of self, comes specifically through the formation of *personal*, affirming love. That is, the formation of persons, in its essence, comes through personal relationships. Seminary structures and rules are meant to facilitate relationships, thus securing not knowledge alone but true understanding.

A man who has been adequately affirmed is capable of revealing to others their own goodness and worth, through his very experience of and affective response to them. This is truly the fruitfulness of human love: it can open one to God's love, in a particular way, in the person of the priest as father. It is not merely what the priest does, but his gift of self which manifests Christ's love for His flock.[14] However, even in his identity as chaste spouse, the priest can hold back, just as does a husband who lives more like a bachelor; his wife experiences his love as lacking, as conditional, rather than fully and freely given. All this man's explanations of why she ought not feel that way are for naught, as the bride senses his selfishness and his holding back the full gift of himself.

She feels unloved for herself and senses the truth that her spouse's real love is for himself more than for her. The flower of love begins to fade, and the relationship becomes arduous. Similarly, the Church will not be able to flourish as fully when a priest does not desire to be the most loving spouse he can be–if he is not willing to sacrifice all for Her (the Church's) sake, as did Christ.

Fatherly Love

Fatherliness requires a development of the heart, meaning that the man guards his interiority so as to remain a man capable of communion with his spouse and children. Fatherly love manifests itself first in the heart of the man called to be father. An earthly father's mission begins by being receptive to the gift of a unique human person who is helpless and who has only needs. Then, it is to protect and serve the child so that the child may live and flourish. An earthly father's role, however, does not end there. All that he does for his child is best accomplished when he *desires* the best for his child, that is, when his *heart* is *moved* with love. Then his actions take on a transcendent character, as long as he remains affectively open to his child and does not allow himself to be caught up only in *doing* things in an effective manner for his child. Without a well-developed interiority where affectivity fuels the heart of the father, the role of father can devolve into rituals of service without love, where the sole focus becomes the effective provision of earthly means, and the father is too spent to be able to be present to spouse and children. Resentment can flourish in this atmosphere, where a man's own focus, thereby, becomes the focus of his children and, in turn, he feels used for what he can provide for their comfort.

On the contrary, the man of communion–because he has been *moved* by the love of others–knows the value of interior movements of the heart and, so, desires this for his children. He jealously leads them along "paths of righteousness" but not in a merely cognitive manner. The man of communion recognizes the importance of his children being moved affectively by the highest truths, so he guards and nurtures their interiority and affectivity.

In the same way, the priest is called to be father, to help the helpless out of a *desire* to help. As Jesus first addressed the hearts of those who were in need and only then gave them the truth, so, too, the priest needs to attend to the hearts of the faithful, and then to teach, exhort, etc. The heart is the fertile ground where Christ may enter; to ignore this detail is to disregard the gift of the person whom God is calling. This is not to say that the priest is never to exhort or correct behavior. Rather, the priest as a man of communion lives affectively, close to the Heart of the Lord. This is the best mode through which a penitent may humbly receive the correction of the priest. The priest's fatherliness allows the Word to penetrate his thoughts and feelings.[15] Then, just as he himself knows what it is like to hear God and be called–for he has experienced the love of the Father–the priest is able to prescind from his own experience to call others as the Father desires: with His own love, tenderness, strength, courage, and wisdom. The priest, as father, seeks not his own will[16] and, therefore, in his dealings with his own parishioners, he treats them as the people of God they are: free and responsible. He recognizes that "authentic Christian obedience (is)...lived without servility,"[17] and, as such, is only inculcated through respect for the subject, having his good at heart.[18]

Spiritual Physician

The interiority of the heart is also essential to the priest who becomes spiritual physician at ordination. As the Divine Physician desires the healing of body, mind, heart, and soul of the Bride, the priest is called to attend to the need for healing within the Church. As spiritual physician, the priest realizes that the *mode* of transmission of healing is just as important as the *matter* of healing and that he, as the embodied Christ, is that "mode."

Christ's healing was not accomplished in a perfunctory manner. Rather, in each case, the Scriptures describe how Jesus encountered each supplicant in a *personal* way, sometimes questioning, sometimes testing, but always responding to the unique person. Jesus further used the material at hand to heal; He used His own spittle to wet the dirt to make mud, applying it to the blind man's eyes. He wrote in the dust as He readied Himself to respond to the Pharisees who were calling for the stoning of the woman caught in adultery. Correcting, guiding, teaching, and healing were all present in Jesus' response to the woman and to the Pharisees.

In a similar way, the healing that Christ brings to each penitent in the Sacraments of Eucharist, Reconciliation, and the Anointing of the Sick comes through the person of the priest who is a man of communion. The *Program of Priestly Formation* notes, "A man of communion [is] a person who has real and deep relational capacities, someone who can enter into genuine dialogue and friendship, a person of true empathy who can understand and know other persons, a person open to others and available to them with a generosity of spirit. The man of communion is capable of making a gift of himself and of receiving the gift of others. This, in fact, requires the full possession of oneself. This life should be one of inner joy and inner peace—signs of self-possession and generosity."[19]

The man of communion who is spiritual physician embodies the love of Christ for His Bride, as he recognizes Him in each person to whom he ministers sacramentally. The priest who possesses himself is able to be present and rejoice with those who desire to know Christ in a deeper way, and who can also be present with those who struggle to know Him. Living out of a reverence for the good, true, and beautiful, and thus guarding his own affectivity, the man of communion is able to guide the faithful to explore distinctions between an external action and an interior movement through which God is speaking. His own affective integration lends itself to a more profound interior sight. As Blaise Pascal said, "the heart has reasons which reason knows not of."

In the sacraments, the priest as spiritual physician brings Christ the Healer to those in need. In the Holy Eucharist, Christ comes as spiritual food, the Bread of Life, to redeem, to reconcile, and to transform the communicant into His own Body.

In the sacrament of Reconciliation, the penitent encounters the Lord's desire to draw him close to His own heart. The priest, as a man of communion, recognizes himself in the penitent, in the sense that he can identify with the humanity of the other and the humility with which the penitent approaches him as confessor. While Christ's own forgiveness is present no matter who the priest is, humility becomes a portal through which the priest assists the penitent to receive Christ's reconciling power. This humility is possible only if the priest is adequately affirmed, and, thereby, capable of opening himself to others and receiving them. Such a man is affectively mature and capable of sensing his own human frailty in those to whom he ministers. The priest, thus, comes *in persona Christi* to exhort, guide, absolve, and strengthen with Christ's own power and authority present to fortify and bring forgiveness and redemption.

In the Anointing of the Sick, once again, the priest as man of communion comes to the infirm person through the laying on of hands. Through physical and spiritual healing with the anointing of oil, the priest as man of communion conveys the curative power of the Holy Spirit through his own person. His presence is that of Christ, the Divine Physician. Thus, his manner reflects the love of the Master Healer.

Good Shepherd

In the ontological change which occurs at ordination, the priest is further imbued with the charism of good shepherd in the image of Jesus as Good Shepherd. This charism is not mere sentimentality utilized to encourage the faithful. The priest as good shepherd is present affectively to others and appreciates the gifts of others without being threatened by them. He is able to exhort the faithful to strengthen and utilize their gifts in the service of their fellow men.

It is to such a pastor that souls may entirely entrust themselves: "Even though I walk through the valley of the shadow of death, I will fear no evil, for you are with me" (Ps 23:4). Coming to know and experience the love and authority of the Divine Shepherd is to journey with the priest who has become the pastor of one's soul, who anoints one with the oil of gladness. It is the man of communion who receives each member of the flock through his affirming presence and sacrificial service, who reveals to them *in his own person* Christ, the Good Shepherd. With due recognition to the objective efficacy of the sacraments, it is through a *person* that souls are formed; it is through *personal*, affirming love of the priest that souls are brought closer to the Heart of Christ.

Conclusion

In conclusion, the Church needs men of communion, men who are self-possessed in the sense of being affectively mature, whose lives are characterized by inner joy and peace. The man of communion guards and nurtures his own affectivity, thereby remaining capable of being present to others. He is able to give himself for the good of others and at the same time, receive the gift of others. Through this inner capacity, this inner maturity and integration of his person, the man of communion becomes a priest who brings *the* Man of Communion–Christ–to the Church. Each member of the Body is, thereby, able to encounter the Head of the Body in a personal way, in a manner which is at one and the same time both affirming and redeeming. This attractive way of being characterizes the man of communion and draws others to Christ through him, enabling them to be healed of their sins and the wounds to their spirits, and to experience the personal love of the Master for them.

The man of communion, having experienced the affirming presence and love of others which gave him a felt sense of his own goodness and worth, recognizes the profound value of living a receptive, open life through affectivity. As a result, he guards and nurtures this way of being in himself so that his intuitive heart remains the guide for his reasoning mind. In this manner, heart and mind function together harmoniously as all the powers of the human psyche are engaged. In turn, the priest who is a man of communion fosters communion in the Body of Christ through his own person, as well as through sacramental ministry.

NOTES

1.   Blessed John Paul II, General Audience (November 14, 1979).

2.   James Keating, "Christ is the Sure Foundation: Priestly Human Formation Completed in and by Spiritual Formation," in *Novo et Vetera*, English ed., 8 no. 4 (2010): 883-99.

3.   United States Conference of Catholic Bishops, *Program of Priestly Formation (PPF)*, 5th ed. (Washington DC: USCCB, 2006), sec. 115.

4.   The Institute for Priestly Formation has come to see the priestly identity as encompassing four realities: Beloved Son, (Mk.1:11) Chaste Spouse, Spiritual Father, Spiritual Physician and Good shepherd. See Blessed John Paul II, *Pastores Dabo Vobis* (1992) where these identities are noted, especially sec. 3 (shepherd and spouse), sec. 60 (spiritual physician); and spiritual father is found particularly in the writings of St. Paul, "I am writing you this not to shame you, but to admonish you as my beloved children. Even if you should have countless guides to Christ, yet you do not have many fathers, for I became your father in Christ Jesus through the gospel" (1 Cor 4:14-15).

See also *Pastores Dabo Vobis* where Blessed John Paul II refers to the priest having spousal qualities: "The gift of self, which is the source and synthesis of pastoral charity, is directed toward the Church. This was true of Christ who 'loved the Church and gave himself up for her' (Eph. 5:25), and the same must be true for the priest. With pastoral charity, which distinguishes the exercise of the priestly ministry as an *amoris officium*,.... he becomes capable of loving the universal Church and that part of it entrusted to him with the deep love of a husband for his wife." (*Pastores Dabo Vobis*, sec. 23).

5.   Pope Emeritus Benedict XVI, Vigil of the 5th World Meeting of Families (2006). http://www.vatican.va/holy_father/ benedict_xvi/speeches/2006/july/documents/hf_ben-xvi_spe_20060708_incontro-festivo_en.html.

6.   Ibid.

7.   Ibid.

8.   Conrad Baars, *I Will Give Them a New Heart* (New York: Society of St. Paul/Alba House, 2008), 43-44.

9.   Ibid, 44.

10.   Conrad Baars & Anna A. Terruwe, *Psychic Wholeness and Healing* (New York: Society of St. Paul/Alba House, 1981), 123.

11.   Conrad Baars, *Born Only Once: The Miracle of Affirmation*, 2nd ed. (Eugene Oregon: Wipf and Stock Publishers, 2012), 23.

12.   Blessed John Paul II, *Love and Responsibility* (San Francisco: Ignatius Press, 1993), 129.

13.   Blessed John Paul II, *Pastores Dabo Vobis* (1992), sec. 25.

14. Ibid, 23.
15. Ibid, 26.
16. Ibid, 28.
17. Ibid.
18. Conrad Baars, *I Will Give Them a New Heart*, 121.
19. United States Conference of Catholic Bishops, *Program of Priestly Formation*, sec. 76.

Attachment and the Formation of the Priestly Identities: Bridges and Barriers

Kathryn M. Benes

In the midst of modern-day confusion regarding priestly identity, Blessed John Paul II reassured the Church that "God promises his people that he will never leave them without shepherds to gather them together and guide them: 'I will set shepherds over them [my sheep] who will care for them, and they shall fear no more, nor be dismayed' (*Jer.* 23.4)."[1] So, it is with great confidence that the holy Catholic Church, through her faithful institutions, seeks to clearly reiterate the identity of her priests, and form them more closely in the image of Christ.

The Institute for Priestly Formation (IPF), an institution founded to assist bishops in the spiritual formation of diocesan seminarians and priests, has come to see the priestly identity as encompassing five realities: (a) Beloved Son, (b) Chaste Spouse, (c) Spiritual Father, (d) Spiritual Physician, and (e) Good Shepherd. These priestly identities are primarily drawn from *Pastores Dabo Vobis*, as well as Holy Scripture.

The five priestly identities provide a broad roadmap for the formation of candidates for priesthood; but what is meant by *identity*, and how is it formed? The etymology of the term "identity" comes from the Latin adjective *idem* (ee-dem) meaning "the same." Therefore, the identity of any particular thing is relational in nature. In order to be "the same," the thing must be compared to something, and suggests a degree of oneness. In regard to priestly formation, the purpose is, through the grace of God, to configure each young man's identity more closely to the identity of Jesus Christ.[2]

Although not formally a part of priestly formation, the *Program of Priestly Formation* (PPF) maintains that the human sciences can serve as a beneficial resource to seminary programs. As such, psychological research indicates that much of the foundational identity of candidates who present themselves for priestly formation will have been formed long before they enter seminary, during their early parent-child relationship. This early formation represents significant bridges or barriers to priestly formation.

A secure attachment between parents and child found in the *first seminary* of the family home serves as a firm natural foundation for the five priestly identities formed in the later seminary of priestly formation. A strong natural attachment, as well as all types of effective human formation, must be rooted in an authentic anthropology that focuses on the flourishing of the human person and gives rise to the person's genuine recognition of being a beloved child of God. Moreover, realization by the seminarian of being a beloved son is essential to the development of the remaining four priestly identities. There are many cultural challenges that threaten a young man's foundational identity, thus compromising his affective maturity and ability to open his heart to the Holy Spirit in order to more fully embrace his priestly identities. When psychological maturity is found lacking in seminarian candidates, priestly formation requires that particular attention be given to specific issues of human formation so that these men are more likely to flourish in their priestly vocation. The science of psychology may be of assistance to seminary formators in this endeavor.

The First Seminary

The *Program of Priestly Formation* states that the, "whole Church receives the gift of vocations from God and is responsible for promoting and discerning vocations."[3] The *PPF* goes on to state that it is "integral to the mission of the Church 'to care for the birth, discernment, and fostering of vocations, particularly those to the priesthood.'"[4] Chief among the various responsible formative entities within the Church is the family. Blessed John Paul II identifies the family as the "first seminary of which children can acquire from the beginning an awareness of piety and prayer and of love for the Church."[5] "[T]he Christian family, in fact, is the first community called to announce the Gospel to the human person during growth and to bring him or her, through a progressive education and catechesis, to *full human and Christian maturity*."[6] He goes on to state that "as an educating community, the family must help man to discern his own vocation and to accept responsibility in the search for greater justice, educating him from the beginning in interpersonal relationships, rich in justice and in love."[7]

The importance of the family's mission to create and foster a community of life and love cannot be overstated. In fact,

Blessed John Paul II wrote in his encyclical *Redemptor Hominis* that "[m]an cannot live without love. He remains a being that is incomprehensible for himself, his life is senseless, if love is not revealed to him, if he does not encounter love, if he does not experience it and make it his own, if he does not partici- pate intimately in it."[8] It is through love, as the "principle and power of communion," that the family becomes who they are called to be, a community of life and love; and, in the midst of this community, each family member *first* realizes his or her identity as a beloved son or daughter of God.[9]

Nature of the Human Person and Christian Anthropology

In order to understand how each person comes to real- ize that he is a beloved child of God, it is important to first understand the nature of the human person based on a sound anthropology. Brugger maintains that "human nature can be described in terms of eight irreducibly distinct but interrelated anthropological facts."[10] He states that humans are: (a) corporal, (b) rational, (c) interpersonally relational, (d) volitional, (e) substantially one, (f) created by God in His image, (g) weakened personally and interpersonally because of sin, and (h) invited to become members of the Body of Christ through faith and Baptism. This anthropology, from a Christian perspective, recognizes the person as both a mate- rial and immaterial being, with natural desires for fulfillment, as well as a longing for transcendence.[11]

Brugger identifies five of the eight anthropological domains, or premises, as philosophical. That is, humans are corporal, rational, relational, volitional, and substantially one. He also outlines three theological premises–specifically, that humans are created in God's image, fallen as a result of sin,

yet redeemed through Christ's perfect gift of sacrifice on
the Cross.

Every means of effective human formation, so critical to
the development of identity, must be rooted in an anthropology that takes into account these aspects of the person. Brugger states that, "although all eight [premises] are necessary for
securing an adequate understanding of the human person,
only one through four are the immediate and variable subject
matter of possible forms of human flourishing."[12] Therefore,
as issues of *human formation* are explored in this paper, the
primary focus will be placed on these four premises:

Corporal

Human persons are corporal, organic beings, engendered
as male or female. They are also creatures with sensation, per-
ception, and memory, who experience emotional responses
and reactions, and are aware of these experiences. The person
is capable of moving himself and can respond to cognitions
and affections in regard to things to be sought and avoided.
Finally, the human person is situated in time and culture
where he has impact and is impacted, but his personhood is
not completely determined by his environment.[13]

Rational

The human person has intelligence and seeks truth and
freedom. He is capable of knowing himself, others, and God.
His knowledge is sensory, perceptual, cognitive, intellectual,
intuitive, discursive, and infused. In addition, the human
person can develop beliefs that involve assent, choice, and
judgment, thus engaging in direct and indirect self-control.[14]

Interpersonally Relational

Humans are social creatures with inclinations and needs for family, friendship, life in society, and other interpersonal relationships. They are receptive and oriented toward others, with the highest expression of interpersonal communication grounded in self-giving. The human person has a natural desire to know, love, and be united with God, his creator and ultimate end. The nature of natural marriage was created in the complementarity of the sexes and the attraction to the opposite sex. Natural marriage is based on life-long commitment and a total gift of self. Interpersonal relationality is first experienced within the family and later extended to friends and the larger community.[15]

Volitional

Humans are capable of responsibility for their actions and have the capacity to shape their moral character, minds, wills, and emotions. In addition, they are capable of loving natural and divine goods and persons. They have the ability to conceive and create, with a tendency toward virtues related to love and justice. Finally, although free, humans are limited in multiple ways and to various degrees in that freedom.[16]

Human Formation

The *telos* of human formation is to facilitate human *flourishing* that, from a Christian perspective, ultimately helps people to attain eternal salvation. When asked, few parents would say that they want to form their children just to "get by." Rather, they would talk about the dreams and high aspirations they have for each child in this world, and a fervent desire that their children share all eternity with the Lord. Similarly, the *PPF* states that "[f]ormation, as the Church understands it, is not the equivalent to a secular sense of schooling or, even less, job training."[17] "Formation is first and foremost cooperation with the grace of God."[18] Moreover, "priestly formation takes place within the context of the Church as the Body of Christ and in relationship to the mission of the Church."[19]

Early Childhood Formation and Attachment

Blessed John Paul II writes that "[a]ll members of the family, each according to his or her own gift, have the grace and responsibility of building, day by day, the communion of persons, making the family "a school of deeper humanity."[20] Pope Emeritus Benedict XVI maintains that it is through this irreplaceable school that "men and women [are able] to grow to the full measure of their humanity. The experience of being loved by their parents helps children to become aware of their dignity as children."[21]

The science of psychology, in regard to early childhood formation, focuses extensively upon the area of attachment theory. Attachment theory is consistent with the Christian anthropology of the human person as outlined by Brugger and supports Blessed John Paul II and Pope Emeritus Benedict XVI in their emphasis on the importance of the family. John Bowlby, a British psychoanalyst, is credited with initially developing attachment theory. He engaged in what was considered a radical trend in philosophy and psychoanalysis that moved away from viewing the individual in intra-psychic isolation toward observing the person within a close relational context.[22]

Attachment, the deep and enduring relationship among

family members and, in particular, between each child and his parents, is at the heart of the family. The healthy relational bonds between parents and children can create a *secure base* from which children can realize their dignity as human persons throughout their lifetime.[23] Conversely, unhealthy relationships between parents and children can result in lifelong relational difficulties far beyond their family of origin.[24]

Secure Base

Healthy attachments between parents and their children can provide a secure base from which children can explore the environment around them, confident in the knowledge that their parents are available to protect them, if necessary. Moreover, healthy parent-child attachment serves as a lifelong secure base.[25] Thus, spousal relationships, as well as adult friendships, provide mutual, relational bases, that are often reflective of the foundational bases, secure and insecure, formed within the family.

The concept of a secure base grew out of Bowlby's interest in parent-child relationships and the manner in which the infant reacted when separated from his or her parents, in particular, the mother. Bowlby hypothesized that, because an infant's survival is dependent upon the protective and nurturing care of the "primary attachment figure," crying and searching for the mother, when separated, was a normal adaptive response. Unlike the predominant thought of his day, Bowlby proposed that the infant's relational experience with parents was crucial in shaping his or her foundational identity and acted as a necessary springboard for the infant to venture forth to discover the world around him or her. In brief, Bowlby maintained that those children whose mothers quickly responded to their physical and emotional needs developed "secure attachments," while the infants whose mothers did not respond effectively to their needs developed "insecure attachments."[26]

Ainsworth later examined individual differences within attachment theory, identifying categories of secure and insecure attachment. Understanding these categories of attachment relationships is critical to all of those responsible for adult human formation, including priestly formation.[27]

Categories of Attachment Relationship

Ainsworth developed a research method to explore attachment behaviors of infants and their parents.[28] This method of research is called the "Infant Strange Situation" (ISS) and has been replicated thousands of times around the world. Ainsworth maintained that the manner in which the parent and child reacted *upon reunification* is reflective of the child's feelings regarding the parent's availability to them, as well as demonstrating the parent's ability to appropriately respond to their child's needs. Her research examines the reciprocal strategies of caretaking and careseeking under stress. Ainsworth concluded that, in addition to secure attachment, there were two categories of insecure attachment; specifically, Insecure/Avoidant and Insecure/Ambivalent. Main and her colleagues later added a third category of insecure attachment, Disorganized/Unresolved.[29]

To better understand the parent's role in the parent-child attachment relationship, Main and Goldwyn developed the Adult Attachment Interview (AAI).[30] The AAI consists of interviewing adults regarding their attachment experiences in childhood. The type of narrative provided by the adult (i.e., coherent or incoherent) was found to be highly predictive of the type of attachment relationship between the adult and his or her parent(s). Secure attachment is reflected by a coherent, clear, and convincing narrative, with insight into parental motivations. Main and her colleagues concluded that an adult who could make sense of what happened in his own childhood, observing the motives of his parents, is likely to respond appropriately to his own child(ren)'s needs, resulting in a secure attachment and, thus, providing a secure base.

In addition to identifying coherent narratives, Main, Kaplan, and Cassidy identified three categories of incoherent narratives: (a) dismissive, (b) preoccupied, and (c) unresolved mourning.[31] The researchers maintain that these three categories of incoherent narratives are predictive of insecure attachment and are similar to one another in that they reflect significant distortions in parent-child relationships.

Secure Attachment (See Table 1)

About two-thirds of children are considered to be securely attached.[32] These children demonstrate a healthy balance between exploratory play away from their parents and a desire to be in close proximity to their parents. For their part, parents of securely attached children tend to be attentive to their child's needs and respond in a non-anxious manner to the communicative messages (e.g., smiles, cries, physical orientation) of the child. These parents generally have a positive outlook on life and demonstrate confidence in their parenting ability.

Insecure Attachment (See Table 1)

Three categories of insecure attachment have been

identified (Avoidant, Ambivalent, and Disorganized) and occur when parenting behaviors are inadequate or inappropriate in meeting the needs of the child.

Insecure/Avoidant (See Table 1)

Approximately 20% of children are considered to demonstrate Insecure/Avoidant attachment style.[33] These children seldom cry when separated from their parent(s) and tend to ignore them upon their return. In some situations, these children will actively avoid their parent(s) after reunification and may avoid eye contact and resist being held.

Parents of children identified with Insecure/Avoidant attachment tend to be indifferent and emotionally unavailable to their child. In some situations, the parent(s) may ignore or actively reject the child when he or she seeks to be comforted.

Insecure/Ambivalent (See Table 1)

Children in the Insecure/Ambivalent category of attachment style make up about 12% of the overall child population[34] and are characterized as anxious even when the parent(s) are present. When separated from their parents, these children become extremely upset and appear somewhat conflicted upon the return of the parent(s), seeking contact while, at the same time, kicking and squirming. They are difficult to comfort and appear fearful to explore their environment in the absence of their parent(s).

Insecure/Ambivalent attachment appears to be associated with an inconsistent parenting style. In addition, exaggerated behaviors in response to the child's attempt to communicate his or her needs, over-stimulation, and ineffective methods of comforting the child can contribute to Insecure/Ambivalent attachment.

Insecure/Disorganized (See Table 1)

Insecure/Disorganized attachment is present in 2% or less of all children.[35] However, up to 80% of children from high-risk families (e.g., abusive parents, drug-addicted parents) are identified in the Insecure/Disorganized category. This attachment style is characterized by disoriented and contradictory behavior. Motor movements and cognitive response times may be slow, and these children may appear clinically depressed. When observed, these children do not appear to have a predictable way of relating to their parent(s) while experiencing separation stress.

Parents of children who are identified with an Insecure/Disorganized attachment style tend to exhibit extremely dysfunctional behaviors (e.g., severely mentally ill, abusive, neglectful). Parents may be frightening to the child. Therefore, when under stress, the child may not know whether it is safe to seek comfort from the person(s) that should provide a secure base for them, or whether they should flee.

Predictive Factors Related to Attachment Categories

Research suggests[36] that children with insecure attachment are likely to experience more difficulties as adults than children with secure attachment; however, using this information in a predictive manner should be done with great caution. Not all children with insecure attachment to their parent(s) develop problems. In fact, insecurely attached children may develop creative relational strategies that contribute in very positive ways to their own development, as well as greatly enhance their relationships. Siegel calls this *earned secure* attachment. Nonetheless, closely assessing early childhood relationships can provide critical information regarding adult patterns of behavior in priestly formation.

Table 1 Features Associated with Attachment Relationships

	Secure	Insecure/ Avoidant	Insecure/ Ambivalent	Disorga- nized/Un- resolved
Occurence in the Child Population	66%	20%	12%	2%
Child's Style (ISS*)	Autonomous	Pseudo-inde- pendent	Demand- ing and/or caregiving to parent	Disorganized
	Secure; Ex- plores readily	Avoids closeness; Attachment behavior deactivated	Attachment behavior over-activated	Becomes controlling or caregiving later
Parent (AAI*)	Responsive; Consistent	Dismissive; Rejecting; Distant	Preoccupied; Entangled; Inconsistent; Intrusive	Frightening; Confus- ing; Fearful; Unresolved mourning
Narrative	Coherent: Free/Secure	Incoherent; denial of past pain; Dismissing	Incoherent: preoccupa- tion with past	Incoherent; Unresolved losses, trauma, or grief
Parental Style	Sensitive and caring: good care planning	Rejecting	Intermittently available	Maltreatment (some)
Relation- ship				
Distance	Free to come and go	Distant	Over-close	Approach/ avoidance conflict (some)

	Secure	Insecure/ Avoidant	Insecure/ Ambivalent	Disorga- nized/Un- resolved
Transaction- al Style	Adaptable	Disengaged	Enmeshed	Chaotic
Relationship (cont.)				
Shared Strategy	Maintains contact; Responds to child when child wants attention	Avoids emotional or physical closeness	Mutual monitor- ing; Blurred boundaries; Role reversal common	No common strategy; Idiosyncratic reunions; Dissociation when fright- ened/fright- ening

*ISS = Infant Strange Situation categories; AAI = Adult Attachment Interview[37]

Interpersonal Neurobiology and Attachment

Daniel Siegel, a prominent contemporary expert in interpersonal neurobiology, whose work has been utilized by the Vatican's Pontifical Council for the Family, makes the case that attachment patterns between parent(s) and child go far deeper than observable behaviors.[38] Siegel emphasizes the importance of viewing the embodied brain as a "social organ," and its healthy development is reliant on interpersonal experiences that are stable across time. The basic relationship between a child and his or her parent(s) helps to establish emotional regulation so that the child can experience the fullness of emotions within and affectively connect with others in his or her external environment. Moreover, the early years of relational life set the groundwork for long-term resilience and mental well-being.

Siegel maintains that the *mind* "emerges from the activity

of the brain, whose structure and function are directly shaped by interpersonal experience."[39] As such, the mind is a "relational and embodied process that regulates the flow of energy and information [biochemical and electrical]."[40] According to Siegel, the development of a foundation for the *neurology of interpersonal experience* is based on three fundamental principles: (a) The human mind emerges from patterns in the flow of energy and information within the brain and *between* brains; (b) The mind is created within the interaction of internal neuro-physiological processes and interpersonal experiences; and (c) The structure and function of the developing brain are determined by how experience, especially within interpersonal relationships, shapes the genetically programmed maturation of the nervous system. Therefore, Siegel's interpersonal neurobiological research supports much of what Bowlby, Ainsworth, and Main learned from their ethological studies on attachment.

Essentially, infants enter the world neurologically "wired" for relationship. The first intimate relationship is typically between mother and child, gradually extending to the father and other family members, and ultimately, establishing the foundation for all other future relationships. As a result of these interpersonal relationships, cells not only in the brain, but throughout the body, develop and change. In fact, Siegel indicates that the "networks of nerve cells around the heart and throughout the body communicate directly with the social parts of our brain and they send that heartfelt sense right up to our middle prefrontal areas."[41] Therefore, a loving relationship can literally change the cells around the heart.

As previously indicated, research shows that these early consistent relationships shape the *mind:* "the relational and embodied process that regulates the flow of energy and information."[42] Secure attachment facilitates *integration*, or the "linkage of differentiated elements of the [neurobiological / brain, mind, interpersonal] system," resulting in healthy functioning.[43] When there is impairment of integration–it is either absent or insufficient–individuals experience emotional *rigidity* or *chaos*. Therefore, attachment impacts the self-regulatory neurobiological circuits that further affects the manner in which an individual interacts with the world around them. With the presence of multiple threats to secure foundational attachment in our contemporary culture, impaired integration of seminarians is sure to be manifested in priestly formation.

Threats to Secure Foundational Attachment

As previously asserted, the family is the first seminary where each person "through a progressive education and catechesis [grows] to full human and Christian maturity."[44] Moreover, the human person cannot live and flourish without experiencing love because otherwise, "he remains a being that is incomprehensible [to] himself."[45]

From a psychological perspective, Bowlby's research on attachment found that "[w]hen the environment deviates too greatly from that presupposed by the master plan…the plan cannot be executed and…[attachment and love] cannot be achieved.[46] Siegel further maintains that the feeling of being attached or loved is related to neurological networks that are formed in the brain very early in childhood development and altering those neural networks becomes increasingly difficult with age.[47]

Given these assumptions presented by both John Paul II and the psychological sciences, it appears that the family is *critical* to the fundamental development of each human person's identity. Thus, deviation from the "master plan" of an early intimate relational environment of "life and love" could significantly compromise the foundational identity formation necessary for seminarians and priests to become who they are called to be as beloved son, chaste spouse, spiritual father, spiritual physician, and good shepherd.

Threats to families and the development of a secure foundational identity are pervasive and well documented. These threats include divorce, single-parent families, child abuse, institutional childcare, technology, media, and the sexualized culture.

With an estimated rate of one in two marriages ending in divorce, (this statistic may be somewhat lower in the Catholic population),[18] it is unquestionably a substantial threat to the security of the family, as a whole and secure attachment of each individual child, in particular. Along with the high divorce rate, more children are currently being raised in single-parent homes than in any other time in our nation's history. Due to the many stressors on single parents, these children also are at risk for insecure attachment. Increasing numbers of applicants to the seminary are coming from divorced and single-parent homes.

Every year, 3.3 million reports of child abuse or neglect are made in the United States. These reports involve nearly 6 million children (a report can include multiple children), and the United States ranks as one of the highest of the industrialized nations for child abuse. Approximately five children die every day due to abuse (80% under the age of 4 years old). The number of abuse-related deaths of children has risen from 3.13 abuse-related deaths per year in 1998 to its current rate today. Far more incidents of child abuse go unreported each year, and this abuse occurs across socio-economic, ethnic, and cultural groups.[49] It goes without saying that child abuse has a significant impact on early childhood attachment and that some individuals who have been victims of child abuse will also be candidates for priestly formation.

In addition to the rise in the number of divorces, single-parent homes, and child abuse incidents that threatens the security of the family, there is another threat; one that is much more insidious and far reaching—early institutionalized childcare. It is estimated that between 61% and 76% of United States children under the age of five are in some sort of non-maternal childcare (this does not include close relatives, such as grandparents, caring for the child). This number has more than tripled over the past 40 years. In fact, children who are four and five years old may be in multiple childcare environments within any given week. To examine the impact of non-maternal childcare, Violato and Russell[50] conducted a meta-analysis of 101 published research studies from 1957 to 1995, consisting of 32,271 children. Although non-maternal childcare did not appear to have a negative impact on cognitive outcomes, Violato and Russell found significant negative effects in regard to the social-emotional, behavioral, and maternal attachment domains. Males tended to fare more poorly across these domains than did females. The researchers concluded that extensive non-maternal care results in negative developmental outcomes for children and may pose a significant threat to society as a whole.

Technology (in particular, excessive use of video games and the Internet), the media, and the sexualized culture also pose significant threats to early childhood attachment. Stepp[51] reports the results of her 10-year research project of the current culture on college-aged youth. She found that about 50% of college-aged adults are "hooking up," defined as "participating in acts ranging from oral sex to sexual intercourse—*every weekend*." Stepp concludes that the "crucial thing to remember in all of this is that hooking up, in the minds of this generation, carries no commitment. Partners hook up with the understanding that however far they go sexually, neither should become romantically involved in any serious way. Hooking up's defining characteristic is the ability to unhook from a partner at any time, just as they might delete an old song on their iPod or an out-of-date email on their computer."[52]

Stepp cites a national study that found that, among eighteen- to twenty-nine-year olds, a little more than a third were in committed relationships. Of those not in committed relationships, most said that they did not want to be. In addition to the lack of commitment in sexual relationships, lack of commitment is also seen in other areas, such as employment histories. Stepp stresses that these young people are not so much a part of the hook-up culture as the unhooked culture. She maintains that, in the final analysis, their non-committal attitude is a pervasive way of thinking about relationships.

According to Stepp, there are three primary contributing factors that must be addressed. First, she maintains that the type of sexualized culture prevalent on television and the Internet promotes the hook-up culture, which leads to mental illness. Secondly, current forms of feminism that masculinize feminine sexual behavior (and feminize masculine behavior) may play a critical role in the hook-up culture. Finally, the busy lifestyles present in the young adult population create the notion that there is no time for relationships and promote the lack of connectedness and commitment to others. Although Stepp did not directly address the issue of attachment disorder as a possible causative factor of the hook-up mentality, the absence of interpersonal connectedness and commitment is the hallmark for insecure attachment disorder.

Cultural Impact on Young Adults

A recent survey of more than 5,000 U.S. adults ages 19-25, published in the December 2008 issue of the Archives of General Psychiatry, found that mental health disorders were common in both college students (46%) and those not attending college (48%). In fact, almost half of the college-age research sample reported having suffered from some type of mental health problem during the 12 months previous to responding to the survey. Interestingly, few sought professional treatment.

Among college students, alcohol abuse and dependency were common at nearly 20%. This was followed by personality disorders (e.g., obsessive-compulsive and paranoid disorders) at 18%. Mood disorders, such as depression and bipolar disorder, were reported in 11% of the college population, followed closely by anxiety disorders.

Another study conducted by the American College Health Association[53] found that nearly half of all college students reported feeling depressed at some point in time, and that almost 15% met the criteria for clinical depression ($n=47,202$). The report indicated that this percentage had increased by 4.6% within a four-year period. The study further indicated that 60% of students reported feeling that things were hopeless at least once during the previous year, with nearly 40% of the men and 50% of the women

reporting that the depression resulted in a functional difficulty (i.e., inability to complete assignments). In addition, the
study indicated that 10% of the students reported seriously
considering taking their lives. It should be noted that suicide
is the third leading cause of death for individuals 15-24 years
(#1 accidents = 46% with 33% automobile accidents; #2
homicides = 15%; #3 suicides = 13%; #4 cancer = 5%).

The socially destabilizing, technologically driven culture
within which youth have become accustomed leaves little
opportunity for the self-reflective and interpersonal face-to-
face interaction that is necessary for the proper development
of the brain, as well as the mind.

Implications for Priestly Formation

The *Program of Priestly Formation* (PPF) outlines the four
pillars of priestly formation developed in *Pastores Dabo Vobis*.
The *PPF* states that "[t]he seminary and its programs foster
the formation of future priests by attending specifically to
their human, spiritual, intellectual, and pastoral formation."[54]
The *PPF* goes on to state that "[c]learly human formation is
the foundation for the other three pillars."[55]

Brugger's descriptive anthropological premises serve as an
excellent "backdrop for existentially situating the human person as a subject of possible mental disorder and flourishing"
within a priestly formation program.[56] In addition, Bowlby's[57]
attachment theory and Siegel's[58] interpersonal neurobiological research provide the basis to advance three fundamental
questions in regard to priestly formation. First, "Can early
relational and neurophysiological development adversely
impact adult identity and behavior in a program of priestly
formation?" Secondly, "How can major relational problems

be identified in candidates who present themselves for priestly formation?" And, finally, "Can attachment barriers to priestly formation be healed, and if so, how?"

Early Attachment and Priestly Identity Formation

The *PPF* states that, "sufficient human formation for admission means not only an absence of serious pathology but also a proven capacity to function competently in ordinary human situations without need to do extensive therapeutic or remedial work to be fully functioning, a psychosexual maturity commensurate with chronological age, a genuine empathy that enables the applicant to connect well and personally with others, a capacity for growth or conversion, and a deep desire to be a man for others in the likeness of Christ."[59] The *PPF* goes on to recognize that, "[i]n contrast to previous generations…today's candidates represent a considerable diversity–not only of differing personal gifts and levels of maturity but also significant cultural differences–that must be taken into account."[60]

This paper clearly outlines the necessity for secure attachment relationship between parent(s) and child, the cultural threats to the development of that relationship, and the ramification of insecure attachment in adulthood. It was previously stated that about two-thirds of the population developed secure attachment.[61] However, more recent related statistics (presented in this paper) may bring that percentage into question. Nonetheless, it may be estimated that roughly two-thirds of the candidates who present themselves for admission to the seminary may be well-adjusted young men. Of the remaining candidates, it is likely that 20% could be classified with Insecure/Avoidant and 12% Insecure/

Ambivalent attachment. Approximately 2% may fall in the category of Insecure/Disorganized attachment. The Disorganized candidates will most likely be initially screened out due to their unusual behavioral history, or because their reported background history is filled with extreme trauma (See Table 1). In addition, a comprehensive psychological evaluation will generally turn up issues that need to be effectively addressed prior to admission into seminary formation.

It is the 32% of candidates who are insecurely attached (either Avoidant or Ambivalent) who are the most difficult to identify, as well as the most difficult for whom to determine whether they are appropriate candidates for priestly formation.

Identification of Relational Barriers to Priestly Formation

The *PPF* states that the, "[a]pplicants must give evidence of an overall personal balance, good moral character, a love for the truth, and proper motivation. This includes the requisite human, moral, spiritual, intellectual, physical, and psychological qualities for priestly ministry."[62] The vocation director and his team serve on behalf of the bishop and presbyterate to determine initially whether the candidate meets the established criteria to move forward in the assessment process. If the candidate meets the initial screening criteria, the *PPF* recommends that a psychological evaluation be conducted to further assist in determining if he should move forward in the admission process. Whether it is the vocation director, his team members, or the psychologist who seeks information, information is typically obtained from personal interviews and evaluations of the candidate alone. Research based on Attachment Theory found that the Adult Attachment Inventory (AAI),[63] when administered to the parent(s), was highly predictive of the child's category of attachment. Although rarely included in a formal way in the admissions process, it would be advisable for the parents of the candidate to become a more critical means of assessing whether the candidate meets admission criteria. Although it would be inappropriate for the vocation director to administer the AAI to the parent(s), the psychologist could administer it in the course of a comprehensive candidate evaluation. Or, a less formal questionnaire could be developed that the vocations director could complete with the parents. In addition, it would be helpful for the AAI to be administered to the candidate during his psychological evaluation in an effort to identify unresolved attachment issues.[64]

The aim of focusing more intensely on attachment issues is to draw on scientific research and expand what is currently being done prior to admission of a candidate into seminary in order to better predict those candidates who are able to be open to priestly formation (i.e., medical/physical assessment, intellectual assessment, and volitional history). Psychological research indicates that early attachment has a profound impact on the adult body (neurobiology), rationality (mind), and volition (will). Moreover, interpersonal relationality is not solely limited to human relationships, but also to God.[65] Grace builds on nature. In order to receive God's perfect self-giving love and understand what it means to be a beloved son, it must first be experienced at a human level. Secure attachment is at the heart of human formation and the five priestly identities.

Compromised Early Attachment and Priestly Identity Formation

The *PPF* states that "the human personality of the priest

is to be a bridge and not an obstacle for others in their meeting with Jesus Christ.... [Therefore], the humanity of the priest is instrumental in mediating the redemptive gifts of Christ to people today....[H]uman formation is the 'necessary foundation' of priestly formation."[66]

When an individual's fundamental identity is significantly compromised by early attachment difficulties, the "necessary foundation" of priestly formation will also be compromised. The *PPF* maintains that "[s]ome patterns of behavior, for example which became set in the candidate's early family history, may impede his relational abilities. Understanding one's psychological history and developing strategies to address elements of negative impact can be very helpful in human formation. This kind of counseling or consultation ought to be distinguished from extensive psychotherapy, which may be needed to address deeply entrenched personal issues that impede full functioning of the person."[67] On the other hand, the *PPF* goes on to state, when "in-depth therapy is necessary, it ought to take place outside of the seminary context prior to the decision concerning admission; or if the necessity for such therapy emerges after admission, then the student ought to withdraw from the program and pursue the therapy before being considered for re-admission to the seminary and resuming his advancement to orders."[68]

It was once thought that neurobiological circuits, laid down in early childhood, were not amenable to change at all. However, one of the most encouraging factors from Siegel's work relates to the *neuroplasticity* of the adult brain or its ability to change as a result of directly shaping patterns of integration.[69]

Siegel[70] maintains that emotional well-being is an

integrated function of the mind, brain, and relationships
(See Figure 1). During early childhood development, this
interpersonal regulation is necessary for survival; however,
throughout a person's lifetime, integration–the linkage of differentiated elements of a system–is needed in order to enjoy a
sense of emotional vitality and well-being; in other words, to
flourish as a human person.

Figure 1 The Triangle of Well Being

MIND   BRAIN

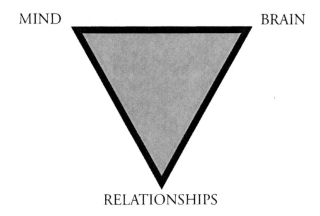

RELATIONSHIPS

Siegel, 2011

Healthy emotional integration is characterized by the
acronym "FACES: Flexible, Adaptive, Coherent, Energized,
and Stable."[71] Siegel compares FACES to the flow of a
"River of Integration," with the central channel being ever-
changing, but, nonetheless, fairly integrative and harmonious.
One of the "banks" of the river represents *chaos*, while the
other bank represents *rigidity*. When a person moves too far
toward the bank of chaos on the River of Integration, his life
becomes unpredictable and out of control. Conversely, when

an individual moves too closely to the bank of rigidity, he becomes emotionally stuck.

Adults who experienced secure attachment in early childhood typically function in the central channel of Siegel's River of Integration. While it is normal for there to be emotional fluctuation, moving in moderate ways toward rigidity or chaos in response to environmental stressors, these individuals do not tend to end up on either bank of the river.

The bank of chaos may be represented by impulsiveness, controlling, negative and provocative behavior, lack of trust, anger and agitation, addictions, helplessness, lack of responsibility and confusion, approach/avoidance interpersonal style, inconsistency. A tendency toward chaotic imbalance may, but not always, represent Insecure/Disorganized Attachment.

Rigidity is typically manifested by an extreme need for control, negative behavior, resistance to love and guidance, avoidance of physical or emotional closeness, lack of trust, superficial positive traits (pseudo-maturity), fear of commitment, and dismissiveness. Rigidity may, but not always, be reflective of an Insecure/Avoidant Attachment.

Insecure/Ambivalent Attachment may be represented by persons moving from one bank to the other on Siegel's River of Integration. These folks may be stuck in a ridged behavior pattern of emotional entanglement/dependency, enmeshment, with blurred boundaries. Insecure/Ambivalent Attachment may also be apparent by intermittent emotional accessibility–sometimes very caring, and at other times, quite demanding or distant.

Siegel's River of Integration serves to describe the range of behaviors that occur as a result of integration of brain functioning (body), mind (rationality), and interpersonal relationships. Healthy integration assists the person in his capacity for freedom (volition) and responsibility to appropriately shape his moral character, as well as his actions related to himself and others. Healthy integration serves as the "necessary foundation" of priestly formation.[72]

Eight Domains of Integration

Siegel[73] identifies eight domains that directly shape a person's degree of integration. These domains are: (a) Integration of Consciousness; (b) Horizontal Integration; (c) Vertical Integration; (d) Memory Integration; (e) Narrative Integration; (f) State Integration; (g) Interpersonal Integration; and (h) Temporal Integration. Although Siegel focuses on the use of psychotherapy to address each of these domains, psychotherapy is necessary only if the seminarian is consistently in a state of rigidity or chaos. The majority of the men in priestly formation are most likely operating in the "central channel" of Siegel's River of Integration and are, therefore, able to work effectively with their program of priestly formation.

Integration of Consciousness

Integration of consciousness is the skill to stabilize attention so that prudent choices and change can be made. This attention enables the seminarian to "acknowledge troubling states without being taken over by them, and to see things as they are, rather than being constrained by …expectations of how they 'should be.'"[74] The effect of this domain of integration is to regulate mood, calm internal upheaval, and develop a flexible and stable mind. Integration of consciousness can be accomplished within formation through instruction, prayer and personal reflection, community life and feedback, as well as work with formators and spiritual directors.[75] Only in extreme cases of inattentiveness should psychotherapy be needed.

Horizontal Integration

The left brain and right brain have separate and complementary functions. The right brain develops early in life and is responsible for "imagery, holistic thinking, nonverbal language, autobiographical memory, and a host of other processes."[76] The left brain develops later and is responsible for "logic, spoken and written language, linearity, lists, and literal thinking." If one side becomes dominate, the linkage between the two sides can become blocked, limiting the complexity that occurs from the two sides working together. Integrating the two hemispheres of the brain harnesses the power of neuroplasticity, giving the person a new sense of his life and deeper insights into himself and others. Horizontal Integration should be addressed by a trained psychologist who could work directly with the seminarian, as well as consult with the formator and/or spiritual director.

Vertical Integration

Siegel states that, "[f]rom head to toe and back again, vertical integration links differentiated [areas of the body] into a functional whole."[77] It can be compromised due to trauma or in adaptation to emotional deprivation. In this state, a person can be cut off from his senses and bodily sensations, leaving him with numbed feelings and perceptions. If extensive trauma, abuse, or neglect is responsible for the person's "numbed out" state, it is best for a mental health professional to work with the seminarian. However, if trauma, abuse, or neglect is not present, the program of priestly formation, along with the wisdom of the formator and/or spiritual director, may be able to assist the seminarian to bring his sensations into awareness and enable him to flourish as a beloved son.

Memory Integration

Layers of memory are the result of processed and encoded experiences.[78] Implicit memory begins in the womb and accounts for much of early childhood experiences. Without intention, emotions, perceptions, actions and bodily sensations shape our expectations of the world. It is important to note that implicit memory can account for a person's actions without his awareness. Generally, implicit memory becomes explicit memory (within the awareness of the person), and the person can live fully in the present. However, early trauma can impair the integration of memory and presents a barrier, resulting in either a rigid state of avoidance or an intrusive state of chaos.[79] In situations such as this, it is necessary for a professional mental health provider to work with the seminarian.

Narrative Integration

Humans try to make sense of their lives by creating stories about themselves. As discussed previously, research shows that the best predictor of a secure attachment is the ability to tell our life story in a coherent manner. Detecting blockages to narrative integration, then examining and making sense of those blockages can move the seminarian toward FACES: Flexible, Adaptive, Coherent, Energized, and Stable.[80] If the blockages are not too extreme, formators and/or spiritual directors can consult with a mental health provider to give them guidelines about working effectively with the seminarian. When the blockages are a result of trauma or neglect, narrative integration should be addressed by a trusted mental health professional.

State Integration

Each person experiences distinct states of being that emerge from fundamental human drives and needs, such as "closeness and solitude, autonomy and independence, caregiving and mastery."[81] When these states are recognized and accepted as natural dimensions of the human experience, state integration is enjoyed. If the person feels that his experienced states are in conflict with one another and he attempts to reject or suppress them, it can lead to emotional instability, resulting in shame or even terror. State integration allows the person to examine past patterns of adaptation and denial and "become open to [his] needs and…meet them in different ways at different times." Depending on the severity of these conflicts, they may be addressed within priestly formation, or in more extreme cases, in the context of psychotherapy.

Interpersonal Integration

The "we" of well-being is the capacity of the brain's resonance circuits to "feel" the internal world of another and vice versa. Past interpersonal experiences may restrict current relationships, inhibiting the seminarian from closely connecting with others. The goal of effective interpersonal integrations is to engage "more intimately in relationships while still retaining our own sense of identity and freedom."[82] Becoming aware of how the past may have shaped the present through neurobiological changes in early childhood can positively impact current dysfunctional relationships. Community life and feedback, as well as work with formators and spiritual directors, can be particularly helpful to improve interpersonal integration. If, however, the level of relational dysfunction is extreme, it may be necessary to consult a trained mental health professional.

Temporal Integration

Temporal integration allows a person to live with ease and draw comfort from connections with others during times of uncertainty. Anxiety regarding death and the uncertainty of life, when there is no present threat, can sometimes lead to obsessions or existential dread that leave the person paralyzed with fear. Obsessive-compulsive disorder is a hardwired survival drive that seeks for control. Due to its physiological base and concurrent psychological impact, temporal integration impairment always requires treatment from medical and mental health professionals.

Conclusions

It is the nurturing love of parents for their young child in the first seminary that draws out the child's identity as a beloved son or daughter. That love provides the security necessary for the child to go forth and become who he is—a child of God. Confident in that "first love," children can grow in affective maturity and freely open their hearts, to be guided by the Holy Spirit, giving their lives totally and unreservedly to Christ.

For all kinds of reasons, cultural and otherwise, that first love may have been compromised, thus impairing that child's fundamental human formation. In fact, the psychological data suggest that increasingly large numbers of young men are likely presenting themselves as candidates for priestly formation with profound emotional and corresponding neurobiological wounds that restrict their ability to offer their lives as a total gift of self. If they do not possess natural secure attachment, it may be difficult for them to freely choose the priestly vocation and fully develop their priestly identities as beloved son, chaste spouse, spiritual father, spiritual physician, and good shepherd. The question then becomes, "Should these young men who seek the priestly vocation be rejected outright?"

The *Program of Priestly Formation* states that some types of counseling or consultation with seminarians can be distinguished from extensive psychotherapy. In these situations, the *Principle of Subsidiarity* should be employed. That is, anything that can be done within the normal structure of seminary formation should be done there. On the other hand, when extensive therapy is necessary, the rector, formators, or spiritual directors should seek the assistance of psychologists to help young men heal broken relationships and develop secure attachments. It is important, however, that these therapeutic interventions be carried out by trusted mental health professionals who fully appreciate and understand sound philosophical and theological anthropology, and grasp the priest's unique ecclesial mission and vocation. In this way, psychology can be brought to the service of the Church.

NOTES

1. Blessed John Paul II, *Pastores Dabo Vobis* (1992), sec. 1.
2. United States Conference of Catholic Bishops, *Program of Priestly Formation*, 5th ed. (Washington, D.C.: USCCB, 2006). secs. 22-23.
3. *Program of Priestly Formation*. sec. 32.
4. Ibid.
5. *Pastores Dabo Vobis*, sec. 41.
6. Blessed John Paul II, *Familiaris Consortio* (1981), sec. 2.
7. Ibid.
8. Blessed John Paul II, *Redemptor Hominis* (1979), sec. 45.
9. *Familiaris Consortio*, secs. 17-18.
10. E. C. Brugger, "Psychology and Christian Anthropology," *Edification* 3, no. 1 (2009): 5.
11. Ibid.
12. Ibid., 7.
13. Institute for the Psychological Sciences, *Model of Integration* (Unpublished manuscript, Arlington, VA, 2012).
14. Ibid.
15. Ibid.
16. Ibid.
17. *Program of Priestly Formation*, sec. 68.
18. Ibid.
19. *Program of Priestly Formation*, sec. 43.
20. *Familiaris Consortio*, sec. 21.
21. Pope Emeritus Benedict XVI, *Family: Spiritual Thoughts Series* (Washington, D.C.: USCCB, 2009), 26.
22. R. Karen, *Becoming Attached: Unfolding the Mystery of the Infant-Mother Bond and Its Impact on Later Life* (New York, NY: Warner Books, 1994).
23. M. D. S. Ainsworth, "Attachments and Other Affectional Bonds Across the Life Cycle," in *Attachment Across the Life Cycle*, ed. C.M. Parkes, J. Stevenson-Hinde, and P. Marris (New York, NY: Routledge, 1991).
24. J. Bowlby, *The Making and Breaking of Affectional Bonds* (London: Tavistock, 1979).
25. Ainsworth, "Attachments and Other Affectional Bonds."
26. Karen.
27. M. D. S. Ainsworth, *Infancy in Uganda: Infant Care and the Growth of Love* (Baltimore: Johns Hopkins University Press, 1967); M. D. S. Ainsworth, "Patterns of Attachment Behavior," in M.D.S. Ainsworth, *Infancy in Uganda* (1967). http://www.psychology.sunysb.edu/attachment/ainsworth/ainsworth_index.html. M. D. S. Ainsworth, *Criteria for Classification of One-year-olds in Terms of the Balance Between Exploratory and Attachment Behavior at Home* (Unpublished manuscript, 1970). Retrieved from http://

www.psychology.sunysb.edu/attachment/; M. D. S. Ainsworth, "Infant-mother Attachment," *American Psychologist* 34, no. 10 (1979): 932-937.

28.   M. D. S. Ainsworth, "Attachment as Related to Mother-Infant Interaction, in *Advances in the Study of Behavior*, ed. J. B. Rosenblatt et al. (NY: Academic Press, 1979), 1-51.

29.   M. Main, N. Kaplan, & J. Cassidy, "Security in Infancy, Childhood, and Adulthood: A Move to the Level of Representation," in *Growing Points of Attachment Theory and Research*, ed. I. Bretherton & E. Waters, *Monographs of the Society for Research in Child Development* 50, no. 1-2 (1985): 66-104.

30.   M. Main & R. Goldwyn, *Adult Attachment Classification System* (Unpublished manuscript, University of California, Berkeley, 1993).

31.   Main, "Security in Infancy, Childhood, and Adulthood."

32.   M. D. S. Ainsworth, M C. Blehar, E. Waters, & S. Wall, *Patterns of Attachment: A Psychological Study of the Strange Situation* (Mahwah, NJ: Lawrence Erlbaum Associates, 1978); M. Main & J. Solomon, "Procedures for Identifying Infants as Disorganized/Disoriented During the Ainsworth Strange Situation," in *Attachment in the Preschool Years*, ed. M.T. Greenberg, D. Cicchetti, & E.M. Cummings (Chicago: University of Chicago Press, 1990), 121-160.

33.   Ibid.

34.   Ibid.

35.   M. Main & J. Solomon, "Procedures for Identifying Infants as Disorganized/Disoriented," 121-160.

36.   D. Siegel, *The Developing Mind: How Relationships and the Brain Interact To Shape Who We Are*, 2nd ed. (New York: Guilford Press, 2012).

37.   J. Byng-Hall, "Creating a Secure Family Base: Some Implications of Attachment Theory for Family Therapy," *Family Process* 34 (1995): 45-58; Siegel, *The Developing Mind.*

38.   Siegel, *The Developing Mind.*

39.   Ibid., 1.

40.   D. Siegel, *Mindsight: The New Science of Personal Transformation* (New York: Bantam Books, 2011), 52.

41.   Ibid., 12.

42.   Ibid., 52.

43.   Ibid., 64.

44.   *Familiaris Consortio*, sec. 2.

45.   *Redemptor Hominis*, sec. 45.

46.   J. Bowlby, *Attachment and loss: Vol. 1. Attachment.* (New York: Basic Books, 1969/1982).

47.   Siegel, *The Developing Mind*; Siegel, *Mindsight.*

48.   G. Barna, *New Marriage and Divorce Statistics Released* (2008). https://www.barna.org/barna-update/article/15-familykids/42-new-marriage-and-divorce-statistics-released.

49.   U.S. Department of Health and Human Services, Administration

for Children and Families, Administration on Children, Youth and Families, Children's Bureau, *Child Maltreatment 2010* (2011). http://www.acf.hhs.gov/programs/cb/stats_research/index.htm#can.

50.   C. Violato & C Russell, "Effects of Nonmaternal Care on Child Development: A Meta-Analysis of Published Research," in *The Changing Family and Child Development*, ed. C. Violato, E. Paolucci-Oddone, & M. Genuis (London: Ashgate Publishing Ltd., 2000), 268 301.

51.   L. S. Stepp, *Unhooked: How Young Women Pursue Sex, Delay Love and Lose at Both* (New York: Riverhead Books, 2007).

52.   Ibid., 5.

53.   American College Health Association, "American College Health Association-National College Health Association (ACHA-NCHA) Spring 2004 Reference Group Data Report (Abridged)," *Journal of American College Health* 54, no. 4 (2004): 201-211.

54.   *Program of Priestly Formation*, sec. 70.

55.   Ibid., 73.

56.   Brugger, "Psychology and Christian Anthropology," 5.

57.   Bowlby, *Attachment*.

58.   Siegel, *The Developing Mind*.

59.   *Program of Priestly Formation*, sec. 37.

60.   Ibid., sec. 38.

61.   Ainsworth, et al., *Patterns of Attachment*.

62.   *Program of Priestly Formation*, sec. 44.

63.   M. Main, E. Hesse, & N. Kaplan, "Predictability of Attachment Behaviour and Representational Processes at 1, 6, and 18 Years of Age: The Berkeley Longitudinal Study," in *Attachment from Infancy to Adulthood*, ed. K.E. Grossmann, K. Grossmann & E. Waters (New York: Guilford Press, 2005), 245-304.

64.   Siegel, *Mindsight*.

65.   Brugger, "Psychology and Christian Anthropology," 5-18.

66.   *Program of Priestly Formation*, sec. 75.

67.   Ibid., sec. 80.

68.   Ibid.

69.   Siegel, *Mindsight*; Siegel, *The Developing Mind*.

70.   Siegel, *Mindsight*.

71.   Ibid., 70.

72.   *Program of Priestly Formation*, sec. 75.

73.   Siegel, *Mindsight*.

74.   Ibid., 71.

75.   *Program of Priestly Formation*, sec. 80.

76.   Siegel, *Mindsight*, 72.

77.   Ibid.

78.   Siegel, *Mindsight*.

79.   Ibid.

80. Ibid.
81. Ibid., 74.
82. Ibid., 75.

IN SERVICE OF PRIESTLY FORMATION: THE CLERGY-PSYCHOLOGIST COLLABORATIVE RELATIONSHIP[1]

ANTONY BOND

The relationship between priests and psychologists has rarely proved simple or lacked contention. In recent years, there has been new interest in the relevance of psychology to priestly formation, stimulated by the publication of the *Guidelines for the Use of Psychology in the Admission and Formation of Candidates for the Priesthood* (hereafter, referred to as "the *Guidelines*").[2] There have been conferences regarding this subject at Alma College in Michigan, as well as those organized by the St. John Vianney Center in Pennsylvania, regular conversations within the newly formed Catholic Psychotherapy Association, and a large-scale study of psychological assessment conducted in 2010 by the National Catholic Educational Association (NCEA) and the Center for Applied Research in the Apostolate (CARA). All of these meetings have brought welcome information on, among other things, the nature of a

Christian anthropology and discussion of developmental markers.

Despite the renewed interest, collaboration "in the field" still remains a mixed affair. A priest colleague who attended one of the conferences above recalled that, halfway through the proceedings, it dawned on him that all the psychologists seemed to be sitting on one side of the room and all of the formators, on the other. When the most enthusiastic collaborators in the country would rather not sit next to one another, there is a problem. If the interaction merely involved an occasional psychological assessment, perhaps this separation would not matter. However, the *Guidelines* require psychologists and formators to work in such a way which involves a significant degree of integration. This integration is a radical notion in the psychological profession and appears to run counter to much current expectation and practice among formators.[3]

What is of interest here is how the anthropological and cultural traditions of the Church and of psychology, as well as questions of individual differences amongst the participants, affect the collaborative relationship itself. In light of the *Guidelines*, the particular focus here is on the nature of "collaborative" interaction—by this is meant relationships which are ongoing and professional, more than the sum of their parts or a financial transaction. They allow for some form of psychological consultation concerning human development and functioning and/or facilitate the assessment and/or psychotherapeutic treatment of candidates for the priesthood. They also offer the potential for a degree of mutual influencing in arriving at conclusions which can be shared or, in some sense, "owned" by both psychologist and formator.

For the sake of brevity, this work concentrates primarily on collaborative relationships in relation to the diocesan priesthood–though the discussion here may be relevant to other collaborative relationships in relation to pastoral concerns, the treatment of priests, and work with religious.[4] The term "psychologist" is used for convenience, given that the majority of interactions with mental health professionals in the area of priestly formation involve assessment and that psychologists are generally the only ones licensed to perform these tests.[5] However, the use of counseling is not uncommon–and may involve other mental health professionals.[6] The term "formator" is used primarily to mean those people with whom psychologists actually work at present–vocation directors, spiritual directors, and those clergy with primary responsibility for human and pastoral formation. This usage is not meant in any way to negate the relevance of relationships to those primarily working in intellectual formation. A consistent theme within Chapter V of *Pastores Dabo Vobis*[7] is that no pillar of formation is discrete. In light of the fragmented nature of the academy, psychologists need ongoing conversations with philosophers and theologians–and it would be hoped something of this would occur through formators, in general. It is necessary to work first within practical constraints of the existing situation and relationships in the hope that the field may expand in its ambition from there.

Foundations of Collaboration

Before looking at problems in the collaborative relationships, it seems helpful to lay some foundations concerning anthropology and historical and cultural traditions.

The primary challenge in any practical collaboration might be said to be created by the unity of the person. In a Christian anthropology, the person is said to be substantially one.[8] There are bodily and spiritual aspects of the person with distinguishable elements–cognition, the life of grace, moral decision-making, brain biochemistry, etc., yet the person is one. In this holistic understanding, each aspect may be said, to some degree, to be dynamic and interrelated, so that change in one may affect another. Many aspects of the person's experience will, therefore, come within the purview of both the formator and psychologist–there are shared areas of interest; the same man is viewed from different perspectives, and each perspective is looking for different things.

A further anthropological challenge is that each person is unique. Individuals are situated in time and a particular environment, fashioned by their own developmental experiences and temperament. Each has his own God-given vocation, shaped by his experiences with God in the life of grace. The essence of "personalness," indeed, has been seen to be "always to point beyond."[9] To approach issues of formation or clinical work is to meet man afresh, with an understanding grounded in theological and philosophical, spiritual and psychological assertions, yet the complexion is always distinct, as is the particular encounter. The person is seen, after all, only in the particular interaction of two unique persons.

In light of a Christian anthropology, one cannot with any accuracy or consistency neatly divide up the areas between the psychologist and formator. In many cases, only a collaborative approach can give the formator the detailed picture that he needs. Yet can each party, psychologist and formator, contribute to a balanced integration, preserving the respective roles and integrity of each within a Christian framework?

In his recent book, *Psychology and Catholicism: Contested Boundaries*,[10] psychologist Robert Kugelman outlines deep-seated traditions across much of the twentieth century that are seen to have produced antagonisms, misunderstandings, and instability in the relationship between psychology and the Catholic Church in America. The priest psychologist Charles A. Curran (not to be confused with Rev. Charles E Curran, the moral theologian) suggested that to be a Catholic psychologist was to be distrusted by psychologist colleagues for being Catholic and shunned by theologian and philosophical colleagues for being a psychologist. Narrowness and defensiveness might be thought the characteristic markers.[11] The literature on collaborative relationships, written either by psychologists or formators, is scarce but what there is relates a tale of collaborators who are all too willing to deviate from a balanced Christian anthropology and to oversimplify and reduce the person.

Early in the relationship between psychology and the Catholic Church, two religious, the psychologists Sr. Annette Walters and her colleague Sr. Kevin (Mary) O'Hara, identified two potential errors in understanding the interaction: first, the secular formulations of psychology may be accepted with insufficient discernment, disregarding the anthropological and moral points of difference; second, psychology may be totally rejected because aspects of it are untrue, thereby negating what it contains of value.[12]

I consider my own training and experience over the last ten years, and I see the confusion and antagonism left whenever these errors have been at play. When I first informed priest friends of mine that I would study clinical psychology,

I was greeted with concern and, at times, a kind of anxious disdain. I was given *Goodbye, Good Men* by Michael Rose, a collection of colorful and disturbing accounts of seminary life. I learned of mental health professionals in the seminary being allotted a role likened to that of psychiatrists in the Soviet Union. A man was sent to therapy for reprogramming to a "party line" of acceptable attitudes by a faculty of the "hard left," and he was very often never seen again. It seemed seeing a psychologist could be compared to being sent to a gulag. I recall being told a somewhat gruesome tale of seminarians being made to sit in a circle on the floor around a religious sister (who was also a therapist) passing around an orange. Each would peel a piece of it off before having to reveal secrets about their sex lives. This activity was begun, in graphic detail, by the nun.

How representative such stories are is, perhaps, less relevant than the existence of a rich and immediately accessible culture of fear and disparagement due to abuses. Of course, a culture of disparagement–with, often, a much higher degree of condescension–exists in psychology with regard to religion. Those student psychologists with an interest in religion come soon to confront the lengthy list of often rather brilliant theorists who assume from the outset that the transcendent is not to be taken seriously on its own terms. For example, the cognitive theorist Albert Ellis, who died only a few years ago, purportedly, was told in a debate that while most clients in America were Christians, most therapists were atheists or agnostics, and this must be leading to mistakes in treatment and probably highly unethical attacks on faith. Ellis remained unmoved: the patients were sick and, therefore, religious; the therapists were healthy and, therefore, were not. He could not change this reality—what more did the questioner want him to say?[13] It was not an approach I found unrepresentative. Early in my training in London, I recall listening to a clinical psychologist who sought to distance clinical practice from the legacy of Sigmund Freud. He struggled for a suitably damning phrase: Freudian thinking was so bizarre and unattractive, he proclaimed, it could only be compared, in all sincerity, to religion. No one at the lecture complained. Freud would have been livid.

There is room for optimism about collaboration. The relationship with, and use of, psychology takes its place in the polarizations of the twentieth century and the confusion of the post-conciliar period in the Church. However, the recent visitation of the seminaries in the United States[14] suggests that a certain stability and sense of balance in institutional identity has been established in seminaries over the last twenty years. There may be the time and willingness to consider anew the prospect of collaboration between psychology and religion. There have been some positive movements in psychology. Multicultural and postmodern sentiments have, for some practitioners and theorists, led to the qualification of the inheritance of early twentieth century positivist structures. The pleasing factor is that clinicians, in particular, have come to find the person simply more mysterious and complex than a natural science paradigm or the dogmas of personality theory have been able to contain. Empirical studies show the association between religion and mental health, in contradiction to the assumptions of many early theorists, to be at worst, neutral, and often, positive.[15] Leading figures, particularly clinicians who take a more relational or "depth" perspective, may recognize the need for a variety of philosophical assumptions about human nature and psychological systems in approaching the person.[16] There are therapists who specialize in religious work that strive to be "receptive to the meanings of psychological difficulties within a broad and transcendent context."[17]

Nevertheless, the process remains so delicate: what happens when the conversation is subject to less than optimal conditions? The Jesuit Norris Clarke pointed out that the collapse of vocations after Vatican II had a deleterious effect on interest in integrative questions within psychology since there were few people left who had the time to take the six-year clinical doctorate and do graduate level work in theology and philosophy.[18] And yet, adding more priest and religious psychologists does not seem to be a practical answer. It is even arguable whether or not it is ideal.[19] One must work from the reality of the situation as it presents itself.

I will propose here that it is necessary for psychologists and formators to develop a relationship grounded in an informed grasp of one another's discipline and regulated by sensitive awareness of the historical, personal, and professional factors which may threaten or distort collaboration. The impact of secularism on contemporary generations of young men renders it necessary to accept the challenge. This work draws upon the body of literature in the field and a small study conducted recently by the author, interviewing formators and the clinicians who work with them.[20] To look in depth at this area is to discover a relationship seemingly filled with ill-tempered conflict, mutual ignorance, and bad faith. It might lead even the most enthusiastic collaborator to experience a kind of learned helplessness. Yet, such distress must be faced. The capacity to consider in print the vicissitudes of what goes on in a relationship must surely be the foundation for any lasting change. Two problematic approaches to collaboration are identified–an over-enthusiasm for the use of psychologists by formators and an under-enthusiasm for their use. The implication is that there is an appropriate use of and place for psychology–an appropriate kind of enthusiasm and way of working together. These ideas emerge through the following discussion, and some of these conclusions are drawn together at the end.

Overenthusiasm in the Collaborative Relationship

From the early days of the use of psychology in formation contexts, it was noted that a seminarian's "emotional problems" may not be a "primary" concern in referrals to a psychologist.[21] This position seems to be true even before Rose's reports of Soviet-style policies of a "hard left" faculty, and is far from unknown after it. A seminarian's ability to accept priestly formation in freedom is always a legitimate topic, and yet is it the case that any seminarian who is willful or who has a big personality is seen by the clinician or formator to have a pathology?[22] In recent times, two formators and a psychologist, Jerome Bracken, John Harvey, and Maria Valdes,[23] observed from their own experience where there is a complaint that a man is insufficiently "pluralistic," the man may suffer from obsessive-compulsive type thinking, yet equally the complaint may also reflect conflicts concerning differences that are generational, theological, or simply the result of a clash of personalities.

Questions arise whether these areas can be effectively separated in the presentation of the seminarian and, if so, is it clear which ones the psychologist is being asked to address?

The seminarian's personality needs to be a bridge and not an obstacle,[24] yet how far might a use of psychology subject him to an inappropriate kind of micromanagement? The temptation to seek to make a man in one's own image, rather than to help him realize his unique vocation in Christ's image, is a subtle but pervasive one in formation and clinical practice.

The lay psychologist Paul Muldoon critiques those formators who "subtly avoid…responsibility" to a candidate by "relying too much" on psychological interventions. He suggests formators neglect the complexity of problems which likely require intervention on multiple levels. What is, perhaps, most interesting of all is that Muldoon admits that he struggles with the temptation to accept this "super human" role and believe psychologists are sufficient and can fulfill such naïve fantasies.[25] Riddick stresses the need for Catholic psychologists to point out the limitations of non-intensive counseling and, often, the need for change on multiple dimensions of formation; seminarians need to have good role models, to be offered supportive healthy relationships, and to feel free to bring problems to reflective and intercessory prayer.[26] Moral and spiritual issues may easily be quickly overlooked in the hope of a "quick fix." In anthropological terms, the man's capacity for self-direction—in this case, responsibility for his own formation, as well as his particular nature and dignity—is being undermined. Problems arise either through ignorance of an appropriate role for psychology or through wishful thinking. In the 2013 Chrism Mass, Pope Francis spoke to the clergy of the danger of pelagianism when "self-help courses" cease being useful and start to undermine an understanding of the role of grace.[27]

In my own study, a number of formators and clinicians

seemed highly enthusiastic about psychology as a tool to tighten their control over seminarians and the formation and discernment process. Some had a palpable anxiety, feeling pressure to gain momentum toward formation goals and to do something to avoid the risks of resurgent scandal. A psychological evaluation would provide a template for growth for each man in his first year of formation. Such an evaluation would be obligatory, with limited alterations, given that the collaborators knew what was best for the seminarian. Rather than providing treatment as such, counselors would be employed largely to unearth more information.

There is, perhaps, something of real value here in the need to take the information provided by assessment seriously. And, yet, there is a tension here. The price of a vocation is the need for it to develop with essential reference to the man's encounter with God. The subjective and experiential dimension cannot be reduced or manipulated.

The counseling relationship between seminarian and psychologist needs to retain a significant degree of client confidentiality. There need to be some limitations wherever the Church is paying for therapy; but if clinicians are to elicit trust and help the men, they need to be more than informers, feeding all information straight back to formation committees. Psychologists and formators need a firm relationship in which the clinician is trusted to be there to help the man in light of a Catholic worldview and understanding of the priesthood and, in the end, place more information into the hands of formators than would otherwise be discovered at all. In the pressures of formation, the danger is that the possibilities offered by assessment and the nature of counseling will be misunderstood.

The ideal is that all seminarians be transparent and trusting of formators. Yet, this ideal supposes a number of things: the seminarians have a significant degree of self-knowledge, openness, and a capacity for self-revelation; and the formators are sufficiently psychologically minded to understand them, a mammoth task for anyone, however experienced. The formation system is worthy of trust, given its evaluative nature and its inevitable struggles to operate in an optimal fashion, yet it may not be at all inviting to place many issues in the external forum and trust that one will be treated sensitively.

Of course, enthusiasm for psychology need not entail being highly directive. Even if sex therapy with oranges is a thing of the past, secular humanism, sometimes integrated into a kind of "psychospirituality," still casts a shadow over the area. This was not a creation of academic psychology, per se, but more a product of a particular mood in the post-conciliar environment. It involved the removal of distinctions and the highly selective blending of elements of faith with a secular humanistic worldview.

The Jesuit psychiatrist Charles Shelton warned that wherever there is an "indiscriminate mixing" of spirituality and humanist psychology, wherein "the subjective self becomes the moral reference point and redemptive suffering is reduced to self-serving victimhood," there is a danger that the Church's understanding of "grace, forgiveness and sin" will be reduced "to mere psychological platitudes."[28] Much has been said about the impact of encounter groups and the effects of Rogerian psychology on seminaries and religious orders.[29] In the contemporary world, there will always remain a danger of a kind of "value neutrality" which promotes autonomy and a secular understanding of freedom as the few absolute therapeutic values. Any gross indulgence of emotional dysfunction so that the will, morality, and personal responsibility are ignored, is a distortion. An approach which can bring such "pleasure…in the additional attention" as to make the seminarian reluctant to abandon the "sick role" must be avoided.[30]

My own study of contemporary attitudes, although on a very small scale, provides little indication that secular humanism is, in itself, a pressing threat. Although most interviewees could recount tales of the overly-sentimental and indulgent use of psychology from twenty or thirty years ago, no one was able or willing to cite an instance of this kind of work in the present time. Perhaps in more rural areas where the choice of psychologists is limited, psychologists promoting secular anthropologies and values remains a problem. And, yet, one of the interesting aspects of the contemporary scene which I uncovered in my study is the existence of Catholic psychologists willing to travel to conduct assessment.

It is interesting to compare the work of Eugene Kennedy, a priest psychologist from Loyola, in Chicago, and that of Monsignor Stephen Rossetti, a priest psychologist currently in Washington, D.C.. Eugene Kennedy spent a number of years as both a psychologist and formator in seminaries in the 1960s and co-authored the famous report on the psychology of priests sponsored by the United States Conference of Catholic Bishops in 1972.[31] The normative picture of human flourishing which was promoted seems decidedly influenced by secular humanism. The report seems subtly to argue against obedience to authority and for barely restrained self-expression, including sexual expression, as an end in itself and mark of psychological maturity. The authors' assumption that the psychological should be isolated from the religious, only to be replaced by secular philosophical assumptions about the person, seems, if nothing else, unhelpful to the Church which commissioned the report. Compare this approach to Monsignor Rossetti's study of the psychology of the priesthood.[32] Rossetti identifies the highest correlation to happiness among the clergy to be the strength of the priest's relationship to God, and, interestingly, the factor most associated with this correlation is the strength of the priest's personal relationships and experience of intimacy supportive of his vocation. Psychological capacities and relational strengths are in a reciprocal relationship with spiritual maturity and devotion. That is helpful integration within a Christian framework.

Perhaps what is most pertinent here is that the misuse of psychology, whether from a secular humanist or behavioral perspective, sets up destructive tensions. It is not that the collaborative relationship will ever be free from tension, but the roles need to be balanced. Both psychologist and formator have responsibility to work from their own specialty but also the responsibility not to negate the role of the other. The psychologist is in the service of the formator but not to the point of compromising the integrity of his discipline or the fundamentals of a Christian anthropology. Ideally, a collaborative relationship should provide a degree of accountability and checks and balances.

Under-Enthusiasm in the Collaborative Relationship

An alternative problem involves the "underuse" of psychologists. This is a more difficult issue, perhaps, and there are multiple aspects to understanding this issue.

It is observed by both formators and psychologists that psychological problems or a serious lack of human flourishing go undetected should individuals simply do what they are told and are "not a problem." Yet, outside the protected structures of the seminary, the seminarian may be exposed. Stress may exacerbate psychological, spiritual, and moral weakness and provoke regression. The terms formators use to describe this condition include seminarians who are "flying under the radar" or who are "submarining" in seminary.

Prior to the Council, psychologists saw docility due to a lack of emotional development, rather than a freely chosen action of submission to authority, as the really serious danger.[33] C. S. Lewis lyrically pointed out in *The Four Loves* that there is a constant danger of "mistaking the decays of nature for the increase of grace."[34] And it seems significant that over 70% of clergy accused of child abuse emerged from a pre conciliar period of formation when docility and passivity seems to have been taken too much at face value.[35] However, it need not involve problems of this magnitude. Lesser emotional or sexual dysfunction may be common; and, indeed, depression may often be hidden in compliance. A lack of interior coherence produces unhappiness, which is only exacerbated by not being expressed. As one psychologist put it, a silent misery too often becomes "the cost of conscious decency."[36]

By its nature, the under-utilization of psychology is difficult to prove here. A study of those who are dispensed from ministry, or are subject to serious emotional or behavioral problems amongst clergy in the five years after ordination, might provide some indication of the scope of the problem, though it would be complicated by a large number of other variables. However, how the problem occurs makes little difference as few dioceses or religious orders appear willing to produce such figures. At the first *A Necessary Conversation* conference, the Jesuit psychologist Fr. McGlone speculated from his own experience that the numbers who either leave the seminary within the first five years or have "severe psychological or sexual misconduct problems" seem likely to be "to the tune of almost, consistently... 20 to 25% of newly ordained clergy."[37]

It is interesting to note that at St John Vianney Seminary in Denver, where counseling is freely available for any man to attend in confidence and there is neither pressure to attend nor not to attend, the psychologist estimates she has seen the majority of seminarians in some capacity during their years at the seminary. Does this mean that every seminarian has a major psychopathology or has somehow been lured into the self-indulgence of secular humanism? No. The psychologist suggests that in a kind of a free market where there is no obligation to come to counseling or not, and the seminarians, formators and spiritual directors would be considered highly orthodox, any therapist who sought to establish a self-indulgent, secular humanist, "therapy culture" would not last five minutes.

Are there, then, some underlying issues and needs among seminarians that are not otherwise being met? Could free and accessible counseling be opening the way for men to address their problems in ways which otherwise would not occur? The therapist at St John Vianney Seminary in Denver is clear in her own mind—the level of interest in counseling is directly attributed to cultural "deterioration," sexual acting out, interpersonal struggles, and developmental failings.

Why Is There Under-Enthusiasm for Collaboration?

Before examining anthropological and cultural factors further, it is valuable to explore the practical elements of collaborative relationships between formators and psychologists. These factors alone might be thought sufficient to make a relationship difficult.

Psychologists cost money though, it might be pointed out, very much less than the human, spiritual, and financial costs associated with only one scandal at a later time, or even with the costs involved in the six-year seminary education of a man who leaves the Priesthood shortly after ordination. Collaboration requires difficult inter-disciplinary conversations. Who has the time or the desire for such conversations? Work in counseling is often preventative, *preventing* the worst behaviors and problems from happening; and this benefit is difficult to quantify or prove. In counseling, psychological work tends to take place in a way which is largely confidential, and this material cannot easily be discussed or defended. Where it is brought to the attention of formators by the seminarian and/or therapist, it is then often the nature of the psychologists' role to reveal a significant number of problems (occasionally strengths) and a lot of unmet needs which often may make the formator's life more difficult.

In priestly formation, it is accepted that each of the people involved in a seminarian's discernment and formation builds on the other's work; but for spiritual directors and psychologists, the truth is not wholly available to scrutiny. There may be evidence of the benefits of therapy in the seminarian's life: a new ease and breadth in his class contributions; a new capacity to internalize and own what he is taught; a new facility to work with others in his pastoral placement; a new depth to his friendships in community; and a new openness and articulateness in his meetings with formators. None of this progress may obviously be attributed to the contribution of the work in counseling. Indeed, in some seminaries, where counseling is available freely and in confidence, few people, if any, may even know that the man is seeing a counselor.

Psychological work lacks certitude in many situations—the human person is highly complex and cannot be reduced to any one formulation or label. Assessment may be expected to bring a useful degree of prediction, as well as a number of hypotheses. However, at times, it may provide no more. McGlone, Ortiz, and Viglione[38] have pointed out the inadequacies of psychological instruments currently available. These instruments are mostly not influenced by a Catholic understanding of normative functioning nor designed to examine the necessary questions and personality features in candidates sought by formators. However, as the authors point out, improvements cannot take place without a culture and tradition of close working relationships with the clergy. The nature of most Catholic universities is such that almost no research in this area has taken place in the psychology departments of Catholic universities since the late 1960s.[39]

On questions of anthropology, formators are right to be concerned; indeed, they must be, if they are to get the best out of collaboration. Even psychologists who are enthusiastic Christians may have uncritically accepted "trends in contemporary psychology" during their training which are based in "anthropological presuppositions that cannot be reconciled with Christian anthropology."[40] One clinician interviewed simply admitted he was "embarrassed for his profession" at the poverty of psychological vocational assessment reports he had read from his colleagues, who seemed both unwilling and incapable of engaging with a Catholic worldview or legitimate requests of the Church. It remains that for all the current enthusiasm for multiculturalism in the psychological profession, philosophy, religion, and spirituality form almost no part of the vast majority of psychology degrees.[41] This phenomenon seems true within Catholic education as elsewhere. An examination of the websites of the psychology departments of most Catholic universities is notable for the way the departments seem to avoid almost any mention of Catholicism. The anthropologies of clinicians may be overly pessimistic and deterministic, or overly humanistic and optimistic.[42] According to the survey of Catholic psychologists conducted by Anna Maria Wallace, there are reported to be a number of psychologists who have personal problems with the faith who would "not be good therapists at all" for work in the field of priestly formation.[43]

The child abuse crisis within the Catholic Church deserves mention here. Although bishops, formators, and psychologists were all criticized in the reports by the John Jay College Research Team[44] and the National Review Board,[45] it has undoubtedly left something of a wound in the Church with regard to psychology. One recently qualified clinician featured in my study recalled "a tongue-lashing" he received from a senior cleric concerning the bad advice the cleric had been given by psychologists–none of whom the clinician had ever even met.

The irony is that it is difficult not to observe that since the Church has been more open to the use of psychology (psychological assessment has become, in effect, necessary), the rate of clergy accused of child abuse has drastically declined. [46] A little known piece of evidence unearthed by the John Jay researchers was that there was significant variety in the numbers of clergy accused of child abuse from different seminaries. The few pre conciliar seminaries which sought to integrate psychology into formation in the 1950s were the ones with the low numbers of clergy accused of child abuse[47]

When psychologists promise more than they can deliver, or collaborations involve or develop a distortion of Christian anthropology, it is easy, perhaps, to become dismissive. Formators may bear the scars of their own experience of secular humanist psychology during formation, have low expectations of psychologists, have limited access to Catholic psychologists, or simply have little knowledge or immediate opportunity of the possibility of working with them.

Unless formators seek proactively to engage with clinicians, the result is often a self-fulfilling prophecy about the usefulness of psychology. Joyce Riddick, a therapist and religious sister who worked on staff in seminaries, noted when cynicism about a clinician's work is repeatedly communicated, "consciously or unconsciously," by vocation directors, staff, faculty, or spiritual directors, it makes the failure of a psychologist very likely, if not inevitable.[48] I found similar sentiments in my survey of clinicians. Unfortunately, seminarians need no encouragement to avoid having to address dysfunctional behaviors or to dismiss psychological evaluations.

Overly distant collaboration is, itself, destructive of the possible benefits and seems to perpetuate antagonism and misunderstanding. Bracken, Valdes and Harvey identify an "exaggerated" respect among both formators and clinicians—a "fear of trespassing on the other person's territory."[49] With inadequate collaboration, "often the spiritual director and the therapist are set in opposition to one another by the directee" in a purposefully manipulative or unconscious fashion. A common scenario is that one or both professionals "back off" a particular problem or intervention because the seminarian tells them that the other has suggested something different[50]. The dynamic thus enables, rather than exposes, defensive maneuvers to substantial progress.

Another example appeared in my own study. A number of the clinicians I interviewed complained of referrals always coming too late. Contact from formators appeared to be a last resort or last chance for a seminarian, with little realistic chance of success given the number of sessions that would be funded. Whether with conscious design or not, the desire seemed to be to confirm and offer validation to preexisting opinions of formators that the man was unsuitable, more than a constructive strategy designed to help him. The result served also to reinforce the notion that counseling is ineffective.

Surely, there are ways of dealing with concerns about the nature of an integrative formulation which involve dialogue and openness. It should be recalled that Catholic psychologists have, at times, been the ones pointing out the threat of secular humanism; and formators have been those who most keenly embrace it.[51] This trend continues today. A clinical colleague, who consults with the Vatican, recently described efforts to combat the naiveté of clergy concerning the anthropology of secular psychologists. Len Sperry warns clergy of the temptation to be intimidated by psychology's claim to be a science and in some sense "value free." He warns against the temptation to succumb to "an age when psychological explanations for complex realities are often uncritically reified and accepted."[52]

It should also be recalled that it is not only psychologists who present anthropological problems or are affected by personal issues with the faith or formation. Few formators would cease engaging with theology or philosophy simply because there are so many dissenting theologians and philosophers.

Interestingly, the following material is largely drawn from formators, clergy, or religious critiquing one another. Bracken, Valdes and Harvey note, "among some spiritual directors there is 'pan spiritualism' which argues that...with grace... prayer and the sacraments alone, the directee will...overcome his psychological difficulties."[53] There are faculty who personally appear "uncomfortable with or feel threatened by the presence of the psychologist."[54] The Jesuit Charles Shelton believes that "lingering feelings of inadequacy" may tempt priests not to make necessary referrals.[55] Riddick reveals she has "serious concerns" about the emotional maturity of some faculty members.[56] Is it, as the Jesuit psychologist and psychiatrist Luigi Rulla proposed long ago, that "the formation of the formators" is, at times, the problem, promoting a vicious circle which bedevils the work of priestly formation?[57] There are those who feel personally threatened by psychological evaluations and tend to dismiss them, in some part because of the fear and anxiety they may feel about their own personal psychological struggles.[58]

Sometimes, vocation directors are accused of being positively unwilling to be discerning. The most common complaint from the clinicians I interviewed was against those who wished the clinician to tell them what they needed to do to "get men through," rather than work with the problems the psychologist observed. Here, the troubled seminarian seems less likely to be "flying under the radar" as "walking in the front door." As the 2010 NCEA report, "Psychological Assessment: The Testing and Screening of Candidates for Admission to the Priesthood in the U.S. Catholic Church,"[59] made clear, the rapid turnover of vocation directors affects the quality of collaboration and assessment. There may also be extreme pressure on vocation directors. They may lack adequate training and struggle to work in multiple pastoral roles in addition to being the vocation director.

Sometimes, the reluctance to engage in collaborative relationships more enthusiastically can take on an institutional flavor. In my survey, one or two formators simply reported that their order or diocese did not accept men with emotional or psychological problems into their seminary and, therefore, they did not need to work with psychologists. Another variant of this position is given by some Catholic physicians from the Linacre Institute,[60] who, in response to the horrors of the child abuse scandal, advocated very stringent standards for entry to seminary–so stringent I wonder whether the Church could weather the exodus from seminaries which would seem likely–at least given the kind of problems I have heard among the men I have seen this year. The physicians appear to hold that the maladjustments of seminarians should either be susceptible to coaching in virtue or to utilizing willpower. Some formators can believe similar things: prayer and moral reasoning are the only real tools for evaluation or formation. The case for coaching in virtue and spiritual direction alone–much, perhaps, as was practiced in the 1950s–is plausible but ultimately mistaken–and it is valuable to explore why.

Formation in a Secular Society

The question facing the Church in contemporary America is whether a seminarian does not need a clear psychopathology to prove unresponsive to formation–he needs only to have been immersed for twenty or thirty years in emotional, moral, and psychological instability–to be, in the somewhat dramatic words of Blessed John Paul II in *Pastores Dabo Vobis*, "imprisoned by an individualistic, materialistic and hedonistic interpretation of human existence."[61] Surveys suggest that around half of all seminarians are now converts or re-verts, those who return to the faith after a period away from it.[62] Indeed, one formator interviewed put the figure at closer to 100 percent of the men in his seminary. Therefore, many of the men can be thought significantly formed "in the world." What does this mean? Gerald Coleman, a psychologist and former seminary rector, reports a pervasive individualism and inappropriate sexualization, particularly through use of the Internet, to be creating serious problems in formation.[63] Len Sperry finds the serious characterological problem of pathological narcissism a deep-seated trait among the young that is flourishing "particularly in the priesthood."[64]

There is a wealth of psychological and sociological material on clinical issues concerning the generation of young adults being produced by contemporary American society. Consider, for instance, a recent article written by two faculty members at Fuller, the major evangelical seminary.[65] In their articulation of some "clinical realities" found by Christian psychologists working with young people, the faculty members name: an erosion of social capital in the relational and emotional resources available to adolescents due to fractured families; an habitual use of technology which produces communication without depth or nuance; expectations from peers or parents which seem increasingly utilitarian, conformist, rigid, and demanding so that life is rarely about the journey but always about competition and production; sexual immorality, sensuality, and pornography which is now *the* mainstream and the norm; and the decline in a capacity for serious self-reflection and reflection about others.

In a recent conversation with a vocation director, he stated that his diocese's priority with regard to choosing a seminary had become human formation. It is not that other areas are unimportant–it is rather that the diocese simply cannot afford to have any more of, what might be termed, "unassignable priests"–those who do not have the personal or interpersonal capacities and psychological stability to take on a responsible job like running a parish. He ran through a number of seminaries which the diocese has used in the past and suggested, in retrospect, that the diocese might not have gone ahead with a number of ordinations, if only they had known the full extent of moral and psychological problems which the man suffered. There was great concern that no one in the diocese or the seminary appeared to be aware of these problems or chose to raise them prior to ordination.

Contemporary neuroscience offers an interesting perspective on the impact of growing up in a secular culture. Bruce Wexler, a neuroscientist at MIT suggests that evidence indicates that experiences which occur in childhood and adolescence create distinct and foundational neural networks that predispose the person to process notions of the self and others in predictable ways. Culture and the social environment play a crucial role in the formation of this filter. Problems occur where there is a radical difference between this way of experiencing and understanding the world and the social environments available later. In childhood, the brain is shaped according to the environment, yet this period of neuroplasticity (the flexibility to create or change neural networks in the brain) is significantly reduced by early adulthood.[66]

In relation to priestly formation, one might wonder what happens when seminarians grow up in a broken, overly narcissistic environment with a Catholic infrastructure that offers a somewhat ambivalent, dissipated, and confused response to secularism. The difference between this environment and that of the Christian community of seminary ought to be radical. If such is to be the case, there will need to be continual assessment of whether the change in environment is beyond the seminarian's capacity to adapt. This is not to reduce the issue to purely developmental or neurological features, or to discount the role of grace and free will; it is to note that it seems more likely seminarians will struggle in societies where a Catholic worldview and understanding of the priesthood appears, in many ways, to be increasingly countercultural.

Complicating the matter, candidates may often lack "the psychological mindedness" or reflective capacities to fully address these questions. The capacity for reflection on oneself and others appears, according to some authorities, to be related to one's capacity for and history of stable, early relationships of loving attachment.[67] An "insecure attachment style" is one way of talking about the kind of problems produced by fragmented social capital–it is seen to impact the capacity to think broadly and limits the person's capacity for intimacy and self-gift.[68] If the rate of divorce among Catholics does not differ from those in the population as a whole, many seminarians seem likely to be insecurely attached.

Interestingly, the literature on contemporary seminarians complains precisely that they seem to be somewhat rigid and inflexible in their thinking.[69] The question must be asked: Does the contemporary seminarian have the desire and capacity for the appearance of natural virtues, but lack the mental infrastructure, literally, the "hard wiring" in the brain, for the necessary integration of will, intellect, and affect to be truly virtuous? Are the early cognitive foundations for a virtuous life, the mental flexibility that facilitates change, and the secure attachment style that allows for deep relationships of self-gift so weak in many candidates that the formation practices of the past are no longer effective?

As indicated, to focus on psychologists alone in the relationship between psychology and religion distorts a Christian anthropology, works against the balanced formulation of the *Guidelines*, and, ultimately, harms collaboration. Formation centers on the life of grace, the influence of formators who can be fathers, the love of the seminary community, the intellectual growth fostered by the faculty, the effects of pastoral experience and prayerful support of the laity, the intercession of the saints, and the spiritual relationships of the men.[70] However, in societies that seem to be forming many young men outside a Christian understanding of human flourishing, efforts in formation can benefit from a close, collaborative relationship with Catholic psychologists to provide consultation and assessment, and, for those who need it, counseling. It is not a question of "either/or" but rather "both/and."

Psychologists have developed helpful clinical approaches to particularly modern problems. What might be termed in formation "affective maturity" finds some psychological correlates in notions of "insecure attachment"[71] and difficulties with "mentalizing"—or the capacity for reflective thought.[72] Psychological techniques of analysis and treatment can be of some assistance here. The importance of relationship, in particular, cannot be underestimated. At times, contact with formators and spiritual directors may simply be, and perhaps inevitably is, too infrequent or general in nature for the needs of some seminarians. Fr. McGlone has suggested there is a gap in the system: "we don't have templates for how to go from internal forum conversations to external forum conversations which are so artificial."[73] For men who are struggling most, the counseling relationship can provide the experience of intimacy and trust, the "supportive authentic relationships that [the priest must] have on a long term basis."[74] According to one clinician interviewed, the problem with the seminarians is that they need to experience what close adult relationships look like and to understand how theirs have been disordered.

Moncher and Titus, a clinician and a theologian, respectively, spent many years attempting to develop virtue (within a Catholic understanding of the term) in therapy with Catholic clients on a Cognitive Behavioral model. In other words, it involved teaching, modeling, behavior, and goal setting. After struggling to make any progress, they discerned that "the majority…are suffering in ways that require immediate and compassionate attention at preliminary levels of motivational, emotional and relational well-being and these must be resolved in order to best situate the person to work with cognitive interventions and finally pursue fuller growth in virtue."[75] The emotional, spiritual, and interpersonal disarray must be dealt with, or broader progress will not occur.

The surveys appear to suggest that issues are not dealt with sufficiently. The priest is, according to Blessed John Paul II, "a man of communion."[76] Yet, sociologist Fr. Hemrick concludes that "the challenge above others" suggested by Dean Hoge's survey of priests,[77] is that there has been a failure of relationship, "a new breed of loneliness."[78] In the latest survey, Gautier, Perl, and Fichter point out: "the one question in our survey that best predicts priest's general happiness is the extent to which loneliness is a problem."[79]

The pastoral reasons are compelling for the importance of relationship. Gautier, Perl and Fichter note that "conflicts with parishioners or laity over issues are a fact of life, and a reality that one in three priests struggle with on a daily basis."[80] If doubters need convincing, it should be recalled that the identifying factor to priests who acted out in the sexual abuse crisis was "intimacy deficits and absences of close personal relationships before and during seminary."[81] Katarina Schuth, one member of the six-person John Jay Research team, concluded recently that a "balanced approach to sexuality and celibacy must be inculcated in future priests by both clerical and lay professionals who are specifically trained in the appropriate disciplines."[82] For formators "to focus purely on pious understandings and practices has not been and will not be a sufficient means of prevention [of child abuse], though some church leaders are voicing concern that this very attitude is gaining prominence."[83]

Are some dioceses, orders, or seminaries really more discerning–with a more virtuous pool of men more resistant to secularism–or are they in ignorance or even denial with regard to the formation challenges which face them? Given developmental realities, men who tend toward insecure attachment, negative views of human nature, and poor relational styles are "not likely to shift" without anything less than a radical intervention.[84] Certainly, there is a case for more pre-seminary lay formation programs, or work with families. Arguably, the existence of such things does not negate the need for collaboration; it simply shifts it to an earlier period.

Seminaries with good Catholic psychologists in adjunct or staff ongoing positions will have a sure ground to flourish. Looking back at the case of the vocation director mentioned earlier, I had a conversation with him about several of the men from his diocese whom I saw in counseling. It was a conversation that neither the seminarians' spiritual directors, restricted by the internal forum, nor formators, who did not know the whole story, were able to have. As a psychologist, with an appropriate release from my client, I could outline to the vocation director the concentrated and structured way the issues of most concern were being addressed. Given the current climate, a major criterion for the success of seminaries will be their capacity to respond to the effects of growing up in an aggressively secular environment.

Conclusion

Mark McMinn, a founding member of the Center for Church-Psychology Collaboration at Wheaton, a Protestant theological college, suggests that where there is a minimum of mutual respect and good communication between religion and psychology, there may be "basic" collaboration.[85] More "advanced" collaboration requires a shared worldview and has greater capacity to affect the system and meet the needs of the Christian community and ministers. A basic level seems currently most common in Catholic dioceses and seminaries. Yet, the *Guidelines* require that, where collaboration occurs, it should be at an advanced level.

Psychologists have an important role to play in service of priestly formation in contemporary America, but it has to be the right kind of psychologist in the right kind of relationship with formators. Psychologists and formators need to be working to bring what is best within contemporary science and the clinical arts within the framework of a Christian anthropology, morality, and understanding of the priesthood, in service of priestly formation.

A relationship of checks and balances within a common worldview and faith offers the necessary framework. It promises a more complete and in-depth understanding of the person and, thereby, more possibilities for effective intervention. The collaborators must in humility desire to better understand the human person—to look, in light of multiple perspectives, at what Walter Farrell termed the "gestalt of man-in-action"[86] and to do so in looking at *this* person, *this* seminarian, in order to help him more freely discern and be open to formation.

The collaborative relationship itself gives evidence, at the heart of priestly formation, to the unity of truth, the possibility of a more coherent approach to modernity, and science, in particular. To be open to dialogue and balance may be thought inherently a very Catholic attitude.[87] It coheres with the vision of Pope Emeritus Benedict XVI in his address at the University of Regensburg[88] and that of Blessed John Paul II in *Ex Corde Ecclesiae*.[89] Inter-disciplinary dialogue seeks not to eradicate distinctions but to understand each discipline in light of Christianity. This approach is not fearful but confident. Indeed, it is ambitious. If this collaboration is not practiced in priestly formation, in seminaries which are, after all, supposed to be "the heart of the diocese,"[90] where will it be accepted?

And, yet, it is not only the principle; it is the practical realities of secular America which should stir formators and psychologists to more constructive relationships. It is simply not enough to rest in the fragmentation of modern society and the contemporary academy. The psychologists Braceland and Farnsworth warned years ago against those faculty and clinicians who would always associate cross-disciplinary dialogue with a "reprehensible," compromised, "less interested" faith or psychological practice.[91] It is seen to emerge from "a basic misunderstanding of the whole human ideal."[92]

What Are the Qualities and Conditions of This Collaboration?

Trust is the "meta-principle" of collaboration,[93] and this trust emerges principally through experience, understanding, relationship, long-term collaborative conversations in openness and respect seeking to help one another grow as Christians seeking the truth. Thomas Merton thought the important element to clergy collaborating with psychologists, which he did as master of scholastics and novices in the 1950s in Gethsemane, was for both sides to cultivate "the humility to remember that no one man is expected to solve all problems—even his own."[94]

Formators set the tone. They are the employers and those responsible for formation. The Jesuits Cucci and Zollner point out that three times the *Guidelines* state that formators must have a good grasp of human psychology—"something which having been so clearly affirmed in the document cannot be ignored."[95] Archbishop Michael Miller, former

Secretary of the Congregation of Catholic Education, states simply that the demands of formation are a "very heavy burden" in the current climate. He suggests "without calling on the help of an expert" who is trained precisely in exploring questions of hidden motivations, the task of a formator is "a very tall order."[96] Fr. German Beorlegui, the Superior of the Jesuit community at the Gregorian University in Rome, examines the complexity of what the responsibility of formation means in practice–the kind of skills it requires–and suggests, finally, that dialogue "between formator and psychologist" where it "includes the Christian conception of the human person" will be an important element of the formator's role.[97]

If formators choose to seek assistance, they should do so with no naiveté about the relationship. There will be tensions; indeed, there must be. The person is too mysterious and the presentation, always fresh and unique. The optimal formation of the seminarian *deserves* problems. Patience and openness are necessary. In a trusting open relationship, formators and psychologists can then learn to be better collaborators *through* the relationship, discovering, perhaps, in an ever deeper way the identity of their own discipline, the necessary distinctions and areas of commonality, a respect for the other, and the unity of knowledge.

The moral theologian Christian Brugger,[98] having spent a number of years working with clinical psychologists in an academic context, produced a paper describing the kind of mind and intellectual habits needed to work in an integrative way. He outlines the concept of an *integrative prudentia*–an embodied way of thinking, feeling, and behaving which allows one to see one's discipline in light of the other without compromising the essence of either. This kind of virtue, like other virtuous aspects to our personalities and character, develops through action, practice, reflection, and perseverance. Interestingly, McMinn[99] studied collaboration between clergy and psychologists in communities of evangelical Christians. The author concludes that ideographic relational factors are, in practice, more important to the clergy than any particular abstract credentials, professional or religious, in establishing collaboration. It is less a question of labels than of the experience of a shared mission and partnership.

Clearly, no collaborative relationship can flourish without time and resources. There are structural issues here. In a Protestant context, McMinn and Wilhoit recommend that psychologists working in collaboration need to receive spiritual formation and theological training.[100] The aggressively secular nature of the psychological profession means that training in clinical psychology in a faith-related context will, perhaps, always be controversial.[101] It is necessary for formators to know the psychologists who possess multiple graduate level degrees and those psychology programs which teach psychology in a context of a Christian worldview.[102] The need for collaboration between psychologically minded formators and spiritually minded psychologists sets up a challenge for dioceses, seminaries, and Catholic universities to provide appropriate training.[103]

Can vocation directors be given the time to concentrate upon vocations, rather than having multiple alternative responsibilities? Can they receive more training? One formator interviewed suggested that radical change in the approach of vocation directors comes about only when they have more experience of the problems of formation and/or coping with the scandals of dysfunctional men after ordination. If such things happen, they take ownership and dispense with a "numbers game." These kinds of changes require bishops to modify their expectations in light of the reality of the dysfunction which is routinely created by growing up in a secular society. The urgent desire for more vocations perhaps needs to be channeled into initiatives to radically impact education, marriage and family preparation and support, and formation in the diocese. This will be the means to allow more vocations to the priesthood to be discerned. In a similar sense, within the seminary, there need to be sufficient numbers of formators so that each can have the time to be a father for his men in formation and time, indeed, to talk to psychologists. The clinicians routinely will be freelance. Unless they are given some kind of adjunct or on-going status, they may simply struggle financially to collaborate.

It is important to note, given the hierarchical nature of the Church, that collaborative relationships can only flourish where a model of openness to collaboration is set by rectors, in particular. Where there is opposition from the top, then no progress is possible. It is one of the principal conclusions in collaborative pastoral projects between psychologists and clergy in Catholic and Episcopalian dioceses.[104]

At a recent conference of formators and psychologists, the Jesuit psychologist Gerry McGlone[105] appealed for an increase in "gospel values" within collaboration. One of the most interesting aspects of my own study was the existence of a number of flourishing relationships. One formator suggested that to support the inevitable difficulties that feature in collaboration, there must be personal relationships deep enough to tolerate the tension. He proposed collaboration must start with each party having a deep personal relationship with God which is allowed to flow into relationships with colleagues. One thinks of the early words of Pope Francis who pointed out that, to be a pontiff was to be literally a "bridge builder" and then equally that "it is not possible to build bridges between people while forgetting God;" and, finally, "it is not possible to establish true links with God, while ignoring other people."[106]

When the *Guidelines* first came out–with their "stunningly integrative" vision[107]–there was widespread skepticism that there could ever be sufficiently psychologically minded formators and spiritually minded psychologists. It was impossible. Yet, the call to collaborative relationship is ultimately a call to conversion of hearts and minds in Christ–to the unity of truth and the centrality of charity to this aim. Fearful, partisan, dismissive interactions are the enemies of truth, most notably the truth that is charity. And, here, collaboration may truly shine–the difficult relationship, the complex engagement, can only be grounded in love. This seems more like the realization of the kind of radically different society which should exist in seminary. What an example such relationships would form for the men who will help shape the Church and society of the future!

NOTES

1. An earlier version of this essay appeared in *Seminary Journal* (Fall 2012). Reprinted with permission.

2. Congregation for Catholic Education, *Guidelines for the Use of Psychology in the Admission and Formation of Candidates for the Priesthood* (2008) (hereafter cited as *Guidelines*).

3. A. Anatrella, *De l'intervention des Psychologues Aupres des Formateurs et des Seminaristes* (2008). http://www.zenit.org/article-19278?l=french.

4. It should be noted that the total number of priests, sisters, and brothers in formation in religious orders is higher than the number of seminarians discerning the diocesan or "secular" priesthood. Further, there is work involving therapy or assessment with priests and religious after ordination or vows. Collaboration with spiritual directors, novice masters and mistresses, and religious superiors is widespread. However, the variety of situations, particularly involving religious orders, each possessing their own "charism, history and mission" is prohibitive for the scope of this paper. United States Conference of Catholic Bishops, *Program of Priestly Formation*, 5th ed. (Washington, D.C.: USCCB, 2006), sec. 30 (hereafter cited as *PPF*). Where the literature on collaboration with religious is thought to be relevant or addresses work both with diocesan clergy and religious, this is included and it is hoped some of the findings may be applicable to analogous collaborative scenarios. However, the focus here is collaboration in the formation of diocesan seminarians.

5. There are no clear statistics on the number of psychological assessments of seminarians taking place; however, the *PPF* requires, in effect, a review of a psychological assessment for all priestly candidates (*PPF*, secs. 39, 47). Assuming the requirements have been followed, the number of assessments in the last five to six years since the fifth edition was published should be somewhere close to the number of seminarians in formation, since on average they take six years or so to ordination. In 2009-2010, the Center for Applied Research in the Apostolate (CARA) estimated there were over 5000 candidates studying for the priesthood at college and major seminaries. Center for Applied Research in the Apostolate, *Catholic Ministry Formation Enrollments: Statistical Overview for 2009-2010* (Washington, D.C., 2010). The National Catholic Educational Association Seminary Department Report on Psychological Assessment surveyed 215 Vocations Director and all reported requiring psychological assessment of all of their candidates. It is "normative" in the US for candidates to undergo psychological assessment. National Catholic Educational Association Seminary Department, *Psychological Assessment: The Testing and Screening of Candidates for Admission to the Priesthood in the U.S. Catholic Church* (NCEA) (Washington, D.C., 2010), 11.

6. A recent survey suggests that three quarters of fifty-eight seminary

rectors in the US indicate that counseling is available via an outside referral and almost one third state it is provided by therapists with some adjunct or on-going status (NCEA). A majority of those connected to seminaries appear to be psychologists but by no means all. A brief survey of the web pages of forty-five seminaries who admit post baccalaureate diocesan seminarians reveals that almost half of them list faculty, staff, or adjunct members with mental health qualifications working in some capacity. The eleven professionals who are cited as having explicitly clinical responsibilities work for eight different seminaries, St. John Vianney, Denver, CO; Mount St. Mary's, MD; St. John's, Camarillo, CA; St. Patrick's, Menlo Park, CA; Christ the King, East Aurora, NY; St Joseph's, Dunwoodie, NY; Our Lady of Providence, RI; St. Mary's at University of St. Thomas, Houston, TX. There are five psychologists, two psychiatrists, two counselors, one marriage and family therapist, and one social worker. The professionals were identified by virtue of their position, qualifications, or biography and the survey undertaken on 07/29/2010. As some of the websites gave very little detail--and anecdotally, it is understood that psychologists work regularly in clinical capacities--for instance at Kenrick Glennon, MO, Holy Apostles, CT, St. Meinrad's, and the Josephinum--it is possible that the true numbers are significantly higher than those readily apparent here.

7.   Blessed John Paul II, *Pastores Dabo Vobis,* (1992).

8.   E. Christian Brugger, "Psychology and Christian Anthropology," *Edification* 3, no. 1 (2009): 5–19.

9.   K. Ware, Foreword, in Bartholomew, the Ecumenical Patriarch, *Encountering the Mystery,* (New York: Doubleday, 2008), x.

10.   Robert Kugelman, *Psychology and Catholicism: Contested Boundaries.* (Cambridge: Cambridge University Press, 2011).

11.   For a full account of the history of the interaction between psychology and the Church, C. K. Gillespie, *Psychology and American Catholicism: From Confession to Therapy?* (New York: Crossroad, 2001) also provides a useful account. In relation to priestly formation, in particular, Len Sperry, "Psychology's Contribution to the Church," in *The Inner Life of Priests,* ed. G. J. McGlone and L. Sperry (Collegeville, MN: Liturgical Press 2012), 30-44, suggests ways in which certain themes in psychology may have impacted priestly formation itself. Chapter 3 of Bond looks at the history of the relationship itself. Antony Bond, *Clinical Consultation and Collaborative Relationships in a Multicultural Setting* (The Institute for the Psychological Sciences: ProQuest Dissertations and Theses, 2012) 374. http://search.proquest.com/docview/ 1266876636?accountid=27532.

12.   A. Walters and K. O'Hara, *Persons and Personality.* (New York: Appleton-Century-Crofts, 1953).

13.   Albert Ellis (1913-2007), one of the foremost psychologists of the twentieth century, described himself as a "probabilistic atheist." He

contributed to a series of famous academic exchanges concerning the relationship between religion and psychology with the Mormon psychologist Allen Bergin in the *Journal of Consulting and Clinical Psychology* and also a number of debates at academic conferences. B.D. Slife and M. Whoolery, "Understanding Disciplinary Significance: The Story of Allen Bergin's 1980 Article on Values," in *The Anatomy of Impact: What has Made the Great Works of Psychology Great?*, ed. R. Sternberg (Washington, D.C.: American Psychological Association, 2003). The charismatic Ellis possessed a characteristically acerbic style of delivery. He was for many years a strident critic of religion--"Obviously...the effective psychotherapist should not...go along with the patient's religious orientation and try to help these patients live successfully with their religions, for this is equivalent to trying to help them live successfully with their emotional illness." Ellis, *The Case Against Religion: A Psychotherapist's View and the Case Against Religiosity* (New Jersey: American Atheist Press 1980), 15. Later, Ellis revised his views to specify more dogmatic, absolutist, or devout expressions of religion or secular values as a problem for mental health. Ellis, "Do I Really Hold that Religiousness Is Irrational and Equivalent to Emotional Disturbance?" *The American Psychologist* 47, no. 3 (1992): 428-29.

14. Congregation for Catholic Education, *Visitation Letter to the Cardinals, Archbishops, Bishops and Major Superiors of the United States of America with Responsibility for Diocesan Seminaries and Religious Houses of Priestly Formation* (2008). http://www.usccb.org/beliefs-and-teachings/vocations/priesthood/priestly-formation/upload/Final-Seminary-Visitation-Report.pdf.

15. James Nelson provides a summary of current research in the role of religion in physical and mental health in chapters 10 and 11 of *Psychology Religion and Spirituality*. "Traditional ideas within psychology that religion is a negative force are generally false. Particularly noteworthy is the destruction of the supposedly scientific view held during much of the twentieth century that organized religion is particularly problematic and to be avoided. In fact research suggests that involvement in institutional religion may be more important to the maintenance of positive...mental health than individual spiritual practices." Nelson, *Psychology, Religion and Spirituality* (New York: Springer. 2009), 390.

16. "My observation [is] most therapists seek to assimilate a diversity of models and metaphors, whether or not they are controversial or conceptually problematic. Effective psychodynamic therapists...mistrust those whose professional identity centers on the defense of one way of thinking and working...[they]...value humility about the extent of contemporary understanding and...appreciate ambiguity and complexity" (N. McWilliams, *Psychoanalytic Diagnosis* (New York:: Guildford, 1990), 20–21.

17. E. P. Shafranske and L. Sperry, *Spiritually Oriented Psychotherapy* (Washington, DC: American Psychological Association, 2005), 25.

18. Kugelman, *Psychology and Catholicism,"* 112.

19.   Some have argued a perceived solution to problems in the relationship is to train sufficient numbers of priestly formators as psychologists
or psychiatrists (Anatrella, *De l'intervention*). The Dominican priest and
collaborator of Carl Jung, Victor White, suggested indeed that there are
particular kinds of complex neuroses "among religious people which only
a priest-psychologist can touch" [White, *God and the Unconscious* (London:
Fontana, 1952/1960), 84]. It is questionable, however, whether it is practical to train sufficient priests in this way, given the demands for mental
health services and drastic decline in numbers of clergy in the US over the
last 40 years, or whether it is desirable with its potential for role confusion
and dual role dilemmas [R. Caplan, *Helping the Helpers to Help: Mental Health
Consultation to Aid Clergymen in Pastoral Work* (New York: Seabury Press,
1972)]. Although clergy, in general, may be thought to be used to choosing or managing multiple roles in the seminary--administrator, spiritual
director, professor, confessor, vocation director, formator, pastor--it might
be wondered whether adding psychologist to the list ought to be avoided
if possible (M. Davies, "When Professors Become Counselors: Ethical
Land Mines in the Seminary," *Theological Education 34*, no. 2 (1998): 9-15).
Further, there is the desire of the Church since Vatican II to promote the
role of the laity in the life of the Church.

A. M. Wallace, summarizing interviews with seven psychologists,
lay and religious, who work with the clergy in therapy, proposes some
advantages and disadvantages to the dual role. Priest psychologists may
"understand the life-style from within" so that there is less need for
explanations. Further "some clients... feel 'safe' with [such] therapists who
'won't take away their faith.'" On the other hand, there is the danger for
the psychologist of "over identification" and a tendency "to assume... too
much and... to moralize" [Wallace, "Initial Encounters of Religious and
Priests with Psychotherapy," The Psychotherapy Patient 1, no. 3 (1985):
156]. Transference issues may be so strong with a priest, the patient and
therapist may struggle to maintain a trusting relationship. Wilson notes
that lay psychologists may be less susceptible to "social pressures," such
as the need to promote priestly vocations and "the will of the superior"
(R.W. Wilson, "Selection of Candidates for Clergy and Religious Life,"
Bulletin of Guild of Catholic Psychiatrists XII, no. 2 (1965): 90). It might
be thought particularly difficult for priest psychologists to be objective
should they be working within their own diocese or religious order.

Others have argued that to purposefully pursue the combination
of the roles diminishes the integrity of the priestly vocation. Early on,
it was noted, "the Church is neither a psychiatric institution nor an
association for mental hygiene" [J.H. Vanderveldt and R.P. Odenwald,
Psychiatry and Catholicism, 2nd ed. (New York: McGraw Hill, 1957),
237]. Although priest psychiatrists and psychologists are useful, they ought
to "always remain a rare exception" (Ibid., 246). In a French Catholic

periodical, it is suggested that Bishops can be reluctant to allow priests to undergo psychological training as it is associated with them leaving the priesthood: "Ils seront même assez nombreux ê quitter le sacerdoce après être passês sur le divan, accréditant le cliché que la "psychanalyse fait perdre la foi" (J. Mercier, "Mon Curé est un Psy.," La Vie (2003). http://www.lavie.fr/archives/2003/05/08/mon-cure-est-un-psy,4542203.php).

There is also an argument that the issues are so complex, the dialogue between psychology and Catholicism is conducted with more clarity when it is external, conducted between two people. Interestingly, a number of the works investigating Catholicism and psychology have been written in the context of a dialogue between priest psychologists and lay mental health professionals: J.R. Cavanagh and J.B. McGoldrick, *Fundamental Psychiatry*, 2nd ed. (Milwaukee: Bruce, 1957); Vanderveldt and Odenwald; F.J. Braceland and M. Stock, *Modern Psychiatry: A Handbook for Believers* (New York: Image Books, 1963/1966).

Notably, the Guidelines require that psychologists are not "part of the formation team" (Guidelines, 6) and formators are not to use "specialized psychological or psychotherapeutic techniques" (Guidelines, 5). This has been interpreted in L'Osservatore Romano to mean no one individual should occupy a dual role (E. Galeffi, "Il Frate Psicologo che Segue i Candidate al Sacerdozio, L'Osservatore Romano (2010). http://www.vatican.va/news_services/or/or_quo/ interviste/2010/081q07d1. html). Perhaps, it might be argued, given the controversies surrounding the use of psychology by certain clergy, greater transparency might be maintained if the conversation between psychology and the faith is played out externally, balanced by and grounded within a relationship.

20. Bond, *Clinical Consultation*. Chapter 5 of the dissertation features an empirical study, involving a small sample of convenience: 10 interviews conducted with formators (vocation directors, spiritual directors, and seminary formators) and clinicians working in the area of priestly formation during 2011–2012. As the participants were asked to provide comment on current working relationships, the interviewees were granted anonymity and any identifying features were removed as a condition of participating in the study. The resultant texts were submitted to analysis using Grounded Theory, a qualitative technique used in sociological and psychological studies. Restrictions on the scale of the study limit the capacity to draw conclusions relating to collaboration as a whole; however, it provides a "snapshot" of the field and a number of hypotheses emerged for further investigation.

21. J. F. Muldoon, "The Role of the Psychologist as Consultant to Religious Communities," *The Catholic Psychological Record* 3, no. 1 (1965): 43.

22. E. C. Kennedy, "Positive Uses of a Psychological Testing Program for Candidates for the Priesthood and Religious Life" in *Psychological Aspects of Spiritual Development*, ed. R. J. Steimel and M. J. O'Brien

(Washington, DC: Catholic University of America Press,1964), 43.

23. C. P. Bracken, M. R. Valdes, and J. F. Harvey, "Spiritual Direction, Therapy and the Directee," *The Linacre Quarterly* 75, no. 3 (2008): 257–64.

24. *Pastores Dabo Vobis*, sec. 43.

25. Muldoon, "The Role of the Psychologist," 49.

26. J. Riddick, "Counseling While in the Seminary" in *Psychology, Counseling and the Seminarian*, ed. R. Wister (Washington, DC: National Catholic Educational Association, 1994), 67-92.

27. Pope Francis, Homily During the Chrism Mass (March 28, 2013). http://www.vatican.va/holy_father/francesco/homilies/2013/documents/papa-francesco_20130328_messa-crismale_en.html.

28. C. Shelton, "Spiritual Direction or Therapy: A Primer for the Perplexed" in *Psychology, Counseling and the Seminarian*, ed. R. Wister (Washington, DC: National Catholic Educational Association, 1994), 43, 47-48.

29. See J. J. Reidy, "Sensitivity Training for Religious" in *Hope: Psychiatry's Commitment. Papers Presented to Leo H. Bartemeier*, ed. A. W. Sipe (New York: Bruner Mazell, 1970); W. R. Coulson, *Full Hearts and Empty Heads: The Price of Certain Recent Programs in Humanistic Psychology* (1994). www.ewtn.com/library/ACADEMIC/FULLHEAR.htm, 215-30; R. Kugelman, "The American Catholic Psychological Association: A Brief History and Analysis," *The Catholic Social Science Review V* (2005): 233–49.

30. Muldoon, "The Role of the Psychologist," 48.

31. E. Kennedy and V. J. Heckler, *The Catholic Priest in the United States: Psychological Investigations* (Washington DC: USCC Publications, 1972).

32. S. Rossetti, "The Priesthood Today and Tomorrow," *Origins* 40, no. 44 (2011): 713–23.

33. P. F. D'Arcy, "Training for the Priesthood Based in Freedom and Responsibility" in *Psychological Aspects of Spiritual Development*, ed. R. J. Steimel and M. J. O'Brien (Washington, DC: Catholic University of America Press, 1964), 80-92.

34. C. S. Lewis, *The Four Loves* (London: Houghton Mifflin Harcourt, 1960/1991), 118.

35. John Jay College Research Team, *The Causes and Context of Clerical Sexual Abuse of Minors by Catholic Priests in the United States, 1950–2010* (2011). http://www.usccb.org/issues-and-action/child-and-youth-protection/upload/The-Causes-and-Context-of-Sexual-Abuse-of-Minors-by-Catholic-Priests-in-the-United-States-1950-2010.pdf.

36. L. E. Hinsie, *The Person in the Body*, (New York: Norton, 1945) in Braceland et al., *Modern Psychiatry*, 281.

37. G. J. McGlone, "Opportunities and Challenges for Ongoing Collaboration Between Psychologists and Catholic Seminary and Formational Staff," a speech given as part of a presentation at the *A Necessary Conversation* conference of priestly formators and psychologists at St. Charles Borromeo Seminary, Philadelphia (DVD recording published by St. John

Vianney Retreat Center/All Occasion Video Productions, June 18, 2010).

38.   G. J. McGlone, F. A. Ortiz and D. J. Viglione, "Cause for Hope and Concern," *Human Development* 30, no. 2 (2009): 12–20.

39.   T. Plante and M. T. Boccaccini, "A Proposed Psychological Assessment Protocol for Applicants to Religious Life in the Roman Catholic Church," *Pastoral Psychology* 46, no. 5 (1998): 363-72.

40.   Blessed John Paul II, *Address to the Tribunal of the Roman Rota* (February 5, 1987), sec. 2. www.vatican.va/holy_father/john_paul_ii/speeches/1987/documents/hf_jp-ii_spe_19870205_roman-rota_en.html.

41.   E. P. Shafranske, "The Religious Dimensions of Patient Care Within Rehabilitation Medicine: The Role of Religious Attitudes, Beliefs, and Professional Practices," in *Faith and health: Psychological perspectives*, ed. T. G. Plante and A. C. Sherman (New York: Guilford Press, 2001), 311-38; D. F. Walker, R. L. Gorsuch and S-Y Tan, "Therapists' Integration of Religion and Spirituality in Counseling: A Meta-analysis," *Counseling and Values 49*, (2004): 69–80.; T. Plante, "A Collaborative Relationship Between Professional Psychology and the Roman Catholic Church: A Case Example and Suggested Principles for Success," *Professional Psychology: Research and Practice* 30, no. 6 (1999): 541–46. Over 80 percent of therapists stated they rarely discussed spiritual or religions issues in training. Walker et al., "Therapists' Integration of Religion and Spirituality in Counseling: A Meta-analysis," 2004. The understanding of vocation in the *Guidelines* "drastically differs" from that with which psychologists are familiar, and there are few places it may be explored in a therapist's development. McGlone et al., "Cause for Hope and Concern," 18.

42.   L. Sperry, "Reclaiming our Catholic Anthropology," in *The Inner Life of Priests*, ed. G. J. McGlone and L. Sperry (Collegeville, MN: Liturgical Press, 2012), 135-43.

43.   Wallace, "Initial Encounters of Religious and Priests," 157.

44.   John Jay College Research Team, *The Causes and Context of Clerical Sexual Abuse of Minors*.

45.   National Review Board, "Report: The Causes and Contexts of the Clergy Sexual Abuse of Minors," *Origins* 33 (2004): 39

46.   The National Review Board identifies the psychosexual screening processes conducted by psychologists with "the significant decrease in reported acts of sexual abuse of minors among priests ordained since 1990" (Ibid., 70). The John Jay Report notes those accused of sex abuse were not "significantly more likely than other priests to have personality or mood disorders," categories picked up by major psychological instruments (John Jay College Research Team, *The Causes and Context of Clerical Sexual Abuse of Minors.*, 3). And yet, abusers do possess distinguishing elements. They are defined by a lack of affective and interpersonal development. There may be personal trauma including victimization as a child, the absence of "close social bonds" or a negative family background,

particularly one repressed about sex (Ibid., 4). Psychologists are trained specifically to reveal, engage, and explore such issues which, if not detected in interviews, are likely to emerge if the seminarians and therapist have time to build close relationships. It is not to suggest that every potential child abuser can be identified, but it does seem, as occurred before Vatican II, it can help [K. Schuth, "A Change in Formation," *America* (January 2, 2012)]. http://www.americamagazine.org/content/article. ctm?article_id=13195. In addition to the question of identification is that of prevention. Psychologists now take an active role in a consultative role in "safe environment" programs in US dioceses. The John Jay Report suggests it was the absence of the availability of "psychological and professional counseling" for child abusers which allowed the pressures to act out to build to the breaking point and not be satisfactorily addressed (John Jay College Research Team, *The Causes and Context of Clerical Sexual Abuse of Minors.*, 3). The report concludes "over the past 25 years" there has been a "remarkable intensification" in the entire area of human formation "in almost every seminary" and psychology has played a role in this. This concentration has coincided with the dramatic decline in allegations of child abuse against the clergy from 975 for the period 1985-1989 to 73 for the period 2004-2008 (Ibid., 47).

47.   Schuth, "A Change in Formation." The sociologist, Sr. Katarina Schuth, one of the team of six researchers employed by the John Jay organization, found intriguing, if anecdotal, evidence for the efficacy of integrated psychological formation programs. The preconciliar generation produced the largest proportion of clergy (70%) accused of child abuse. Those accused were present in much higher proportions in some seminaries than others. Although the lack of comprehensive histories of formation programs and the complexity of the causation of abuse restricts the extent to which conclusions can be drawn, the few psychologically informed seminaries with human formation type programs are correlated with very low numbers of allegations of abuse. One seminary is highlighted as having an innovative faculty in the 1950s. "Unlike most other seminaries at the time," it came "more and more" to give "great weight to psychological assessment as an admissions criterion" supporting "the provision of psychiatric services" for students. Evidence illustrates the rejection of some students and the dismissal of others "because of the attention given to...psychological health." And this seminary is notable for a "long history of very low rates of sexual abuse of minors among its graduates." Another seminary had a moderate number of graduates accused of child abuse initially. However, coinciding with the introduction of a psychologically informed human formation program, this seminary experienced a drop in accusations "significantly before most other schools experienced the same decline."

Although records are scarce, it may be thought highly

improbable, given the rigidity of seminary training and theology prior to the Council, that this involved the psychospirituality and secular humanism seen in the 1970s. The psychology developed in Catholic universities in the 1950s and early 1960s was required to consider the integrative implications with faith. Although psychologists felt hampered by the restrictions of the neoscholastic system, this period before and during the Council may be thought, in retrospect, a productive one in America in terms of developing psychological assessment and clinical practice in light of Catholicism. (See Kugelman, Psychology and Catholicism; Plante et al., "A Proposed Psychological Assessment Protocol," 363-72).

48. Riddick, "Counseling While in the Seminary," 81.
49. Bracken et al., "Spiritual Direction," 257.
50. Ibid., 258.
51. C. W. Baars and A. A. Terruwe, "How to Treat and Prevent the Crisis in the Priesthood," in *I Will Give Them a New Heart: Reflections on the Priesthood and the Renewal of the Church*, ed. S. M. Baars and B. N. Shayne (Staten Island, NY: St Paul's, 1971/2008), 1-26; C. W. Baars, "Whatever Happened to Religious Life,?" in *I Will Give Them a New Heart: Reflections on the Priesthood and the Renewal of the Church*, ed. S. M. Baars and B. N. Shayne (Staten Island, NY: St Paul's, 1978/2008), 1-26; P. Vitz, *Psychology as Religion: The Cult of Self-worship* (New York: Eerdmans, 1977/1994). The psychiatrists Conrad Baars and Anna Terruwe gave an address to the 1971 World Synod of Bishops which discussed the priesthood and was, according to Pope Paul VI, "a gift to the Church." Baars "Whatever Happened to Religious Life,?" xix. Like the work of Kennedy et al., *The Catholic Priest in the United States*, the address was a product of the new interest in psychology after Vatican II which identified a psychological component in the "crisis" of the priesthood and saw the need for a new focus on human formation rather than therapy. And, yet, the work of Baars and Terruwe is important precisely because it is compatible with orthodox Catholic views. They proposed that formators needed to operate as true spiritual fathers, neither through infantilization of seminarians or authoritarianism, nor through sentimentality and indulgence, but rather through mature, responsible love. The ability of priests "to affirm and practice the love of restraint" is seen to be a "deciding factor" for the choice of formators (Baars et al., "How to Treat and Prevent the Crisis in the Priesthood," 26). The vision includes the need for formators to help build spiritual relationships of love. The psychiatrists made clear the confusion regarding sexuality and doctrine in the seminaries in the 1970s had no psychological justification. Love does not involve an "intellectual floundering" through the "abandonment" of religious practices, nor permission for seminarians "to behave as they please," practices which Baars notes in seminaries (Ibid). Indeed, this kind of license is seen to perpetuate a neglect, a lack

of appropriate love which only ensures that the seminarian who lacks affective maturity is made worse. Because love concerns self-gift more than self-expression, celibacy is not a problem of itself. Clinical observations suggests "beyond doubt" that "the emotionally mature priest's freely chosen celibate state makes his love of men and women more beautiful and intense and immeasurably enriches the fruits of his ministry." Indeed, the authors see a clear parallel between the "permanent continence" of celibacy and the "periodic continence required in marriage" (Ibid., 20). It is necessary for formators to develop an "authentic anthropology of Thomas Aquinas, updated and enlarged by our clinical studies and to be wary of most mental health professionals who do not possess this" (Baars, "Whatever Happened to Religious Life,?" 45; Baars et al., "How to Treat and Prevent the Crisis in the Priesthood," 1971/2008, 24).

52.   L. Sperry, *Ministry and Community* (Collegeville, MN: Liturgical Press, 2000), 1.

53.   Bracken et al., "Spiritual Direction," 259.

54.   Riddick, "Counseling While in the Seminary," 81.

55.   Shelton, "Spiritual Direction or Therapy," 61.

56.   Riddick, "Counseling While in the Seminary," 90.

57.   L. M. Rulla, *Anthropology of Christian Vocation.* Vol. 1 (Rome: Gregorian University Press, 1986).

58.   Bond, "Clinical Consultation," 264.

59.   NCEA, *Psychological Assessment.*

60.   *After Asceticism: Sex, Prayer and Deviant Priests* (Bloomington, IN: Linacre Institute, 2006).

61.   *Pastores Dabo Vobis*, sec. 8.

62.   G. Coleman, *Catholic Priesthood, Formation and Development* (Ligouri, Missouri: Ligouri Publications, 2006); D. R. Hoge, *Experiences of Priests Ordained Five to Nine Years* (Washington, DC: National Catholic Educational Association, 2006).

63.   Coleman, *Catholic Priesthood.*

64.   Len Sperry, "The Psyche and Soul: Personality and Spirituality," in *The Inner Life of Priests*, ed. G. J. McGlone and L. Sperry (Collegeville, MN: Liturgical Press 2012), 123.

65.   C. Clark and D. Clark, "Connecting and Serving Today's Adolescent," *Christian Counseling Today* 18, no. 2 (2011): 37-39.

66.   B. Wexler, *Brain and Culture* (Boston: MIT Press, 2007).

67.   A. W. Bateman and P. Fonagy, *Handbook of Mentalizing in Mental Health Practice* (Arlington, VA: American Psychiatric Association, 2011).

68.   Attachment Theory was developed by a British psychoanalyst, John Bowlby (1907-1990). It is an empirical and biologically based theory which suggests that experience of close emotional relationships (or the lack of them) throughout life, though particularly during early childhood, shapes the way people subsequently think, feel, and behave, often doing

so at an implicit and unarticulated level [Bowlby, *A Secure Base: Parent-child Attachment and Healthy Human Development* (New York: Basic Books, 1988)]. It was developed in part from the scientific observation that pre-verbal children (aged two to three years) appeared to have predictable patterns of emotional regulation and behavior in response to caregivers, according to the kind of parenting which had occurred up until that time. An "insecure" style of attachment has been found to be strongly correlated with psychosocial problems and psychopathology. See M. Mikulincer and P. R. Shaver, *Attachment in Adulthood* (New York: Guilford, 2007) or Len Sperry has a helpful brief summary. Sperry, "Reclaiming our Catholic Anthropology," 139–141.

69. Coleman complains seminarians "suffer from a narrow technological education" with "little exposure to the humanities," which leaves them lacking "a certain imagination." *Catholic Priesthood*, 21. Jeremiah McCarthy notes often candidates come with "a debilitating form of rigidity in ordinary interpersonal encounters and pastoral settings" [J. McCarthy, "Reflections from a Former Seminary Rector," in M. L.Gautier, P. M. Perl and S. J. Fichter, *Same Call, Different Men: The Evolution of the Priesthood since Vatican II* (Collegeville, MN: Liturgical Press, 2012), 211)]. Munroe suggests that at the deepest level it appears to come down to a limited ability to be adaptive, to think flexibly and broadly [T. Munroe, "Hidden Challenge of Taking up the Role of Pastoral Leader," in D. R. Hoge, *Experiences of Priests Ordained Five to Nine Years* (Washington, DC: National Catholic Educational Association, 2006), 153–65]. Existing degrees often seem to be in the secular field such as business, science, or technology (Schuth, "A Change in Formation"). Schuth notes that the seminarians who were converts and re-verts appeared somewhat fearful or vulnerable about losing what they had gained (Ibid). Hoge agrees that the converts "tend to be somewhat inflexible…since they desire security and stability in their newfound faith" ("Experiences of Priests," 12).

70. The Catholic psychiatrist Conrad Baars provided early evidence in the psychological case for the need for formators to be a "father" to the men, making up for any lack of appropriate sense of self-worth, which might be considered also in terms of "secure attachment." Two leading researchers in attachment theory suggest there is a "positive side of religion that Freud failed to emphasize:" "faith in 'stronger and wiser forces'" in the form of "close relationship partners" or of "figures and forces [such as] God" that help generate "felt security" (Mikulincer et al., *Attachment*, 469). Interestingly, one study has considered how the prospect of a loving relationship with God and the Saints can promote secure attachment (P. Vitz and C. Lynch, "Therese of Lisieux from the Perspective of Attachment Theory and Separation Anxiety," *The International Journal for the Psychology of Religion 17*, no. 1 (2007): 61–80).

71. D. Wallin, *Attachment in Psychotherapy* (New York: Guilford, 2007).

72. Bateman et al., *Handbook of Mentalizing*.

73. G. J. McGlone, "Opportunities and Challenges for Ongoing Collaboration Between Psychologists and Catholic Seminary and Formational Staff," a speech given as part of a presentation at the *A Necessary Conversation* conference of priestly formators and psychologists at St. Charles Borromeo Seminary, Philadelphia (DVD recording published by St. John Vianney Retreat Center/All Occasion Video Productions, June 18, 2010).

74. McGlone, "Opportunities and Challenges."

75. F. Moncher, and C. Titus, "Foundations for a Psychotherapy of Virtue: An Integrated Catholic Perspective," *Journal of Psychology and Christianity* 28 (2009): 23.

76. *Pastores Dabo Vobis*, sec. 43.

77. Hoge, *Experiences of Priests*.

78. E. Hemrick, Forward, in Hoge, *Experiences of Priests*, ix.

79. Gautier et al., *Same Call, Different Men*, 68.

80. Ibid., 76.

81. John Jay College Research Team, *The Causes and Context of Clerical Sexual Abuse of Minors*, 5.

82. Schuth, "A Change in Formation."

83. Ibid.

84. Sperry, "Reclaiming our Catholic Anthropology," 143.

85. M. R. McMinn, D. C. Aikins, and R. A. Lish, "Basic and Advanced Competence in Collaborating with Clergy," *Professional Psychology: Research and Practice* 34 (2003): 197–202.

86. W. Farrell, "A Philosopher's Comment on Foregoing Chapter," in *Psychodynamics of Personality Development*, ed. W. J. Devlin (New York: Alba House,1964), 21-22.

87. Catholicism has been formulated as a religion of "both and" rather than "either or:" "not nature *or* grace...not reason *or* faith...not law *or* Gospel...not Scripture *or* tradition...not faith *or* works...not freedom *or* authority...not unity *or* diversity" [McBrien, *Catholicism: New Study Edition* (New York: Harper Collins, 1994) p. 1190; cited in M. Donahue, "Catholicism and Religious Experience" in *Handbook of Religious Experience*, ed. R. W. Hood (Birmingham Alabama: Religious Education Press, 1995), 37]. There are truths placed in a "constantly shifting and counterbalancing dance" (Ibid).

88. Pope Emeritus Benedict XVI, *Three Stages in the Program of Dehellenization: Address at the University of Regensburg* (September 9-14, 2006). www.vatican.va/holy_father/benedict_xvi/speeches/2006/september/documents/hf_ben-xvi_spe_20060912_university-regensburg_en.html.

89. Blessed John Paul II, *Ex Corde Ecclesiae* (1990). http://www.vatican.va/holy_father/john_paul_ii/ apost_constitutions/documents/hf_jp-ii_apc_15081990_ex-corde-ecclesiae_en.html.

90. Pope Paul VI, *Optatam Totius* (1965), sec. 5.

91.   F. J. Braceland and D. Farnsworth, *Psychiatry, the Clergy and Pastoral Counseling* (Collegeville, MN: Institute for Mental Health, 1969), 4.
92.   Ibid.
93.   M. R. McMinn, J. Ammons, B. R. McLaughlin, C. Williamson, J. W. Griffin, C. R. Fitzsimmons, and B. Spires, "Collaborate with Whom? Clergy Responses to Psychologist Characteristics, in *Psychology and the Church*, ed. M. R. McMinn and A. W. Dominquez (Hauppauge, NY: Nova Science Publishers, 2005), 9-17.
94.   Thomas Merton, 19. Merton T. (1956/1991), "The Neurotic Personality in Monastic Life," *The Merton Annual 4*, 5-19.
95.   G. Cucci and H. Zollner, *La psicologia nella formazione al sacerdozio. La Civiltà Cattolica*, I, (2009), 253.
96.   M. J. Miller, "The Catholic Church's View of the Role of Psychology in Seminary Formation," presentation given on June 14th, 2010, at *The Necessary Conversation* conference of priestly formators and psychologists at St Charles Borromeo Seminary, Philadelphia. DVD recording published by St John Vianney Retreat Center/All Occasion Video Productions.
97.   The formator needs to develop psychological sensitivities–such as the capacity to discern patterns of emotional emphasis in speech and behavior or assess for a capacity to tolerate frustration. He must be able to evaluate psychological diagnosis and prognosis, to detect psychological problems by examining a seminarian's "internal coherence and…stability" and to establish "more effective psychologically formative instruments for...psychoaffective growth" [G. A. Beorlegui, "La Preparacion Psicologica Adecuado," *Seminarium* 2-3 (2009): 397-99]. Beorlegui reminds formators that "the signs of the Spirit are not incomprehensible elements." Rather, they "resonate in the humanity of the individual" (Ibid., 401-402). While warning against "the irons" of secular hermeneutics which plague psychology, Beorlegui advocates the "very useful" dialogue with a psychologist where it is truly founded in "the Christian conception of the person...and demands of discernment and formation" (Ibid., 417).
98.   E. C. Brugger, "Christian Integrative Reasoning: Reflections on the Nature of Integrating Clinical Psychology with Catholic Theology and Philosophy," *The Catholic Social Science Review* 13 (2008): 129–67.
99.   McMinn et al., "Collaborate with Whom?"
100.   McMinn, Mark and James C. Wilhoit. 1996. "Becoming Spiritually Sensitive." *Christian Counseling Today*. 4 (1): 21-25.
101.   C.D. Campbell, "APA Accreditation of Doctoral Psychology Programs in Christian Universities," *Journal of Psychology and Theology*, 39 (2011), 59-67.
102.   The Institute for the Psychological Sciences in Arlington, Virginia, is an accredited Catholic institution offering doctorates in clinical psychology. Franciscan University of Steubenville offers a Masters in Counseling. There is the Institute for Psychology at the Gregorian University in Rome.

There are a number of Protestant institutions offering accredited Christian based doctorates in clinical psychology, most notably Fuller Theological Seminary in California, Wheaton in Illinois, and Regent in Virginia.

103.   *Guidelines*, 6.

104.   K. M. Benes, J.M. Walsh, M.R. McMinn, A.W. Aikins, "Psychology and the Church: An Exemplar of Psychologist-Clergy Collaboration," *Professional Psychology Research and Practice*, 31 (5), 515-520; Caplan, *Helping the Helpers to Help*.

105.   McGlone, "Opportunities and Challenges."

106.   Pope Francis, *Homily During the Chrism Mass*.

107.   McGlone et al., "Cause for Hope and Concern," 14.

Out of the New Normal: Jesus Is Calling Men of Communion

Christina P. Lynch

The "New Normal"

"If God is taken out of the equation, then the human person has no human dignity, and we can do with the human person whatever we feel should be done to him or to her regardless of him or her being made in the image and likeness of God."[1]

The removal of God has become part of the "new normal" culture. Over the last several years, cultural agendas have been gradually eliminating the idea of God as our creator and, thus, the dignity of the human person has been reduced to more of an object than a person. This removal of God and religiously cherished doctrines constitutes the new normal in western culture.

Jesus is calling young men into seminary from out of this cultural new normal. Taking into consideration that the

culture has affected these men whom Jesus calls, a proposal
will be made to show how promoting the virtues in seminary
formation can help men move away from the "new normal"
culture and embrace the healing that communion with the
Trinity can give. From this intimate communion, men can
be formed in a fundamental, relational way as priests who
are beloved sons, chaste spouses, spiritual fathers, spiritual
physicians, and good shepherds. It is these identities which
give rise to the diocesan priest's mission. Unceasing union
and intimacy with Christ ignite in the man a desire to choose
good and, ultimately, lead a holy life with a burning desire
to be a saint. The characteristics of a virtuous life will be
outlined and correlated to growth in the priestly identities[2]
as a baseline measure for one becoming a *man of communion*.
Benchmarks for measurement in each virtue can serve as a
guide for formators to assess candidates' readiness at three
time periods in formation.[3]

What is Normal?

Pope Emeritus Benedict XVI reminds us of what is truly
normal in a culture and challenges us to defend it as truth:
"Fellow defenders of true marriage choose your words wisely.
Don't join the rest of the world in declaring what is true to be
merely traditional. We do not call abortion 'choice' because
it is never a moral choice. It is murder. Two persons of the
same gender cannot enter into marriage. It is ontologically
impossible. So it's quite silly for us to begin describing marriage as 'traditional' vs. 'same-sex' because it's drawing a distinction between marriage and something that can never even
exist in the first place."[4]

Critical deviations in values and attitudes over the last

several decades have changed this country's emerging adults' dispositions from one of excellence to adequacy, optimism to pessimism, concern for the common good to concern for individual advantage, delayed gratification to instant gratification, respect to incivility, Christian God to Amorphous God, knowledge to experience, heroes to celebrities, trust to skepticism, and, most importantly, truth to tolerance.[5]

It is from this world view that today's youth are being formed and, predictably, are developing a confused sense of identity and self-worth. Their experiences and lives are "great barometers of the condition of the adult world that is socializing them."[6]

A recent research study[7] on today's emerging adults (18-27) reveals some alarming results. The researchers describe a world view of extensive moral relativism, a lack of engagement in civic endeavors, an apparent lack of freedom for youth who search desperately to discover meaning in their lives, and a failure of society to provide healthy resources to help them find life's true meaning. There is also additional evidence of lower levels of empathy in today's youth. "College kids today are about 40 percent lower in empathy than their counterparts of 20 or 30 years ago, as measured by standard tests of this personality trait."[8] This decline in the ability to be empathic to others can be correlated with the recent rise of social media. "The ease of having 'friends' online might make people more likely to just tune out when they don't feel like responding to others' problems, a behavior that could carry over offline."[9]

"In today's new normal culture the average emerging adult is exposed to three times as much information via the media. In terms of media content, emerging adults have grown up with video games, and a growing body of research is establishing that exposure to violent media numbs people to the pain of others."[10]

These social scientists boldly outline the contrasting values in their research findings. They link to their discoveries five alarming trends in today's emerging adults that take them away from certain natural virtues necessary for healthy development in affective maturity.

1. Morally Adrift

The research states that almost no emerging adult today is able to find deep and lasting meaning to life in the future and, as a result, can live only for today and the instant gratification which brings temporary meaning in the moment. As a result, the truth is based on one's own experience (good or bad), leaving no room for discussion or dialogue. To lead a good life, it is important for people to be able to have constructive discussions about moral differences with those who disagree with their own view. This requires being able to take into consideration how different assumptions shape moral beliefs. "Almost no emerging adult today is able to do that."[11]

2. Captive to Consumerism

Virtuous ideals and behaviors are lacking for many emerging adults as they tend to focus almost exclusively on materialistic consumption and financial security as their guiding principles. The research indicates that emerging adults lack a natural desire to focus on developing relationships that are loving and lasting, pursuing education in the spiritual truths and values, understanding true contentment and generosity, and giving eagerly of themselves in service for the well-being of other people. To lead a good life, it is important for people to understand and hold values that go beyond the acquisition of material things driven by mass consumerism.

3. Intoxication's "Fake Feeling of Happiness"

Developmentally immature emerging adults report frequent, if not habitual or addictive, use of alcohol or drugs or both. The researchers cite outcomes of alcohol and drug abuse as leading to many bad consequences including, but not limited to, date rape, alcohol poisoning, drunk driving, and even accidental death. They note that intoxication and binge drinking by young adults is too common and not even recognized by them as a problem. There is a definitive *disconnect* between their awareness of potential consequences for their behaviors and their actions. Emerging adults are convinced that they do not have an alcohol problem because they believe they can stop drinking at will. But they do not equate consuming multiple (five or more) drinks in a short period of time to be a problem, even if there are adverse consequences. To lead a good life, it is important for people to "avoid a lifestyle of routine intoxication."[12]

4. The Shadow Side of Sexual Liberation

The "new normal" cultural world view destroys the good of sex by exploitation, coercion, or pure self-gratification. In the research studies, the majority of emerging adults have little awareness of the true understanding of the moral good of sex. 85% of emerging adults willingly touched another person's private areas or have been touched by another under their clothes; 71% have had oral sex; 73% have had sexual intercourse; and the average age of the first experience of sexual intercourse is 16 years old. A significant number of the emerging adults reported in the study that this sexual freedom has led to real hurt, confusion, grief, anger, and regret, if not severe suffering and long term harm; however, *they admitted that to protect their sense of personal self (self is sacred) they often deny their regret.*[13] Being allowed to "be yourself" is, by their definition, the ultimate good. In order to protect their physical, mental, and emotional health in intimate relationships, it is important for young people to learn to discern what leads to human flourishing and what causes harm.

5. Civic and Political Disengagement

Most emerging adults, with some exceptions, have little investment in, or hope for, the larger world around them. To lead a good life, it is good for "people to care about the larger social, cultural, institutional, and political world around them."[14] In order to understand oneself as part of a larger civic order that needs to be nourished and regenerated, living the good life requires care for one's neighbors, fellow citizens, strangers, and even enemies. This sense of belonging is important in knowing oneself and one's place in society and can give meaning to life and hope for the future.

If one would draw a picture of today's emerging adult and what is considered the new normal baseline from which young men are being called to discern their vocation, it may look like the crucified face of Jesus. The face of youth today shows great hardship at so young an age. These young people's lives are "complex, fraught with difficulty, often scourged with big problems, serious confusions, and misplaced values and devotions."[15] The causes of their struggles are numerous. There appears to be a lack of elementary reasoning abilities for sorting out basic moral questions; poor decision-making regarding sexual encounters has led to serious harm; and lack of education in discovering and actuating the virtues in their lives has left the impression that the good life involves material possessions and mass consumerism with limited vision of what the future can hold. In addition, the increased role of intoxication and addictions among emerging adults has created an illusion of happiness and has led to a life of stress, anxiety, boredom, and regret with brief relief. This new normal advocating selfism (self as sacred) has created a world view that includes deep detachment from any personal commitment to give of oneself for the interest of others and one's country. Such attitudes of selfism can lead to hopelessness and lack of hope that the future holds meaning when self-seeking desires are not met.

Selfism Versus Self-Giving

The first step in seminary formation is to create a culture in which a man can recover from the secular culture and begin to heal any vicious residue still affecting him. What is most vital to concentrate upon in human formation, therefore, is the development of virtue. Creating a virtuous environment in seminary can help replace cultural attitudes ordered toward selfism and instill attitudes of gratitude, self-giving, and desire to live as men of communion; then, healing and growth in the formation of the priestly identities can occur.

Virtues are the qualities of the human personality that can move people away from selfism and toward consistent good behavior and self-giving. The Catechism of the Catholic Church defines virtue as a "habitual and firm disposition to do the good."[16] "The virtuous person tends toward the good with all his sensory and spiritual powers; he pursues the good and chooses it in concrete actions."[17] Living a virtuous life allows the person not only to perform good acts, but to give to others the very best of himself without regrets. This is a true definition of *a man of communion*. "The ultimate goal of the virtuous life is to become like God."[18]

To become like God! Is that not what priestly formation is about: forming men in priestly identities to become *"in persona Christi Capitis?"*[19] Therefore, if this is the true goal of seminary formation, how do we measure a man's character development as part of his priestly formation?

Living a Virtuous Life

Human (natural) virtues are stable dispositions of the intellect and the will that govern our acts, order our passions, and guide our conduct in accordance with reason and faith. They make possible ease, self-mastery, and joy in leading a morally good life.[20] Dietrich von Hildebrand states that virtue is the quality of someone's character.[21] He argues that virtue is present, even when it is not functioning, and exists in the very core of the person. Virtues must, therefore, be realized to be functioning in a person's life.

Hildebrand's argument presumes that the person has a cohesive sense of self in order to realize these virtues. Therefore, if we think of love as self-gift, to what extent can people give themselves in love when they do not have a cohesive self to begin with? As psychiatrist and Thomistic philosophy professor Rudolf Allers writes in *Forming Character in Adolescents*:

> One cannot give away what one has not got; a person not feeling sure of being or having a true self cannot

but recoil from any situation which would imply such a giving away of the self. A person, furthermore, who has just begun to get hold, so to say, of his self and is still not certain of his possession, cannot be expected to make a gift of this self, because he feels that nothing would be left to him, and that he would fall back into the state bordering on nothingness from which he has just recently, after long and painful struggles, emerged.[22]

One of the characteristics of today's new normal culture is substantial difficulty in the formation of a healthy and cohesive sense of self.[23]

Natural virtues are typically handed on by the environment, especially the home environment, so that those observing them as normal can eagerly embrace them. Given that man is wounded by sin, it takes human effort, and a cohesive sense of self, to embrace the virtues. Today's cultural "new normal" has the tendency to relativize virtues; therefore, the development of virtues throughout life requires intentional perseverance, education, and *mentoring* by wiser adults (in seminary, this role falls to formators, spiritual directors, psychologists, faculty, and the rector), so that human effort can then be purified and elevated by divine grace.

Perseverance and repeated efforts of practice of the good build moral character and help men develop patterns of good behavior so they can become disposed to live a virtuous life and become men of communion.[24] Formators and those assisting in the formation of seminarians need to help men realize that the virtues they already have present in their character can become actualized through daily healthy choices of good behaviors.

While all virtues call us to do good, the infusion of supernatural grace elevates the natural virtues so that it is one's reliance on God's grace that maintains him. The supernatural virtues allow the Father to "refashion hearts into living images of the Heart of His Beloved Son."[25] Virtues, therefore, are part of the mysterious reality of what makes a human being human, and, with the infusion of supernatural grace, give him a desire and a capacity to be a saint.[26]

Jesus of Nazareth, who was fully human, "discloses the human potential for virtue and goodness" and gives us a measurable benchmark for growth in character development in priestly formation. When Jesus was asked by one of the scribes which is the greatest commandment, He replied, " 'Hear, O Israel! The Lord our God is Lord alone! You shall love the Lord your God with all your heart, with all your soul, with all your mind, and with all your strength.' The second is this: 'You shall love your neighbor as yourself'" (Mk 12: 29-31). When the scribe understood this saying, Jesus commented to him: "'You are not far from the kingdom of God'"(Mk 12: 34).

The Theological Virtues and Formation in the Priestly Identities

Faith

How does living a virtuous life help men to grow in the priestly identities? In faith, the hope of God's love that we are created in His image and are His adopted children gives birth to the first and foundational priestly identity: *Beloved Sonship.*

The virtue of *faith* is fundamental to receiving the identity of beloved son. "Do we believe in a God who has created us in his own image and likeness and who has destined us for eternity, an eternity with him or without him? Who breathed

into us an immortal soul which gives us identity and personhood, and can hold the very life of God imparted to us in
the comparable gift called sanctifying grace? ...Without
faith there is no meaning, no drive, no reason"[27] to life. No
meaning, no drive, no reason to live—Is that not the sentiment
described by the majority of young emerging adults from the
"new normal" culture? Vocation directors need to assess that
a candidate applying to seminary can articulate meaning in his
life with Christ, prove his drive is for Christ and his fellow man,
and be able to demonstrate right reason in choosing to enter
seminary formation as part of his discernment to priesthood.

Faith requires a renunciation of arrogance, as well as
self-critical and judgmental thoughts. "This journey towards
humility, towards spiritual childhood is essential," as Cardinal
Dolan noted in reference to Pope Emeritus Benedict XVI.[28]
The renunciation of an attitude of arrogance in which one
knows better allows the "soul to grow and the sensitivity of
the heart to grow towards God."[29] The human heart must be
continually stretched to receive the love of the Father as His
beloved son. As the human heart is stretched into a deeper
intimacy with Christ in the identity of beloved son, the virtue
of faith will continue to burn. As a man identifies with being
a beloved son of the Father, he will find comfort in his own
sexuality and will come to understand better his own mascu-
linity. This acceptance of himself and witness to others will
form him into being a beloved brother by his community.
The more his heart is stretched in intimacy with the Trinity
and Mary, the deeper his own spiritual life will become, thus
helping him to integrate his human sexuality to be drawn to
Christ. This desire to be alone with Christ will help lessen his
own fear of loneliness.

Given that formators need to support and encourage seminarians in their faith, formators ought to know each man personally, spend quality time with him individually and in group settings, and witness his ability to live out the virtues of faith, hope, and love in his daily choices and interactions.

Charity

Christ's gift of himself to his Church, the fruit of his love, is described in terms of that unique gift of self—made by the Bridegroom to the Bride…The priest is called to be the living image of Jesus Christ, the Spouse of the Church…In virtue of his configuration to Christ, the head and shepherd, the priest stands in this spousal relationship with regard to the community…In his spiritual life, therefore, he is called to live out Christ's spousal love toward the Church, his Bride. Therefore, the priest's life ought to radiate this spousal character which demands that he be a witness to Christ's spousal love.[30]

The new normal culture promotes a selfism that increases the struggle with the passions. This grasping to satisfy self discourages self-giving and bearing good fruit that is required in any love relationship. Selfism is different than the self-love Jesus commanded. Loving self is the ability to love the Holy Spirit who dwells in us which allows us to give that love to our neighbor. Love of self knows that we are loved as beloved sons and daughters. Without this knowledge or experience of love, we live in a world of self, seeking worldly love but never quite finding it. Psychiatrists and psychologists agree that most people who seek counseling feel unlovable and are unable to love and respect themselves, let alone their neighbor or spouse.

Benjamin Franklin's autobiography can help seminarians and formators move from a character of selfism to true character of self-love. Franklin was steadfast in cultivating his own character development. He studied his own disposition (knew himself) and made note of his good qualities and the tendencies to evil that he possessed. He developed a plan of formation to root out faults and cultivate virtues.[31] Each week, Franklin worked on a particular fault and noted it in his journal so that he could record, at the end of the week, the increase or decrease of the fault. Simultaneously, he chose to associate with those who were wise and virtuous (good mentors), and he engaged in academic study of the desired virtue. By cultivating good habits and securing a favorable environment, he demonstrated how a man can mold his own character.

Hope

The virtue of hope makes a man capable of living a life of charity, a hope that transcends daily life so that he does not expect success in his earthly days but looks forward to the the fulfillment of the promises of God in eternity. It is only in this extension of the soul, in this self-transcendence, that a man's life becomes great and that he is able to bear fruit despite the effort and disappointments of everyday life, and that he can be kind to others without expecting any reward.[32]

How can formation encourage hope in seminarians? Research has shown that one's environment can influence character and personality development, as well as give hope for meaning in one's life. Promoting an environment of beauty in the seminary culture can help seminarians learn to distinguish between true beauty and the illusion of beauty.

A culture of beauty can help transform men's distorted thoughts about creation to right-ordered reasoning of a loving Creator of beauty. It can give hope to men that they, too, can, with God's grace and mercy, overcome the temptations of the world and be saints.

Seminaries have a responsibility to have good art prominently displayed that can lift the seminarian's soul to God. Images of Jesus and the saints in the role of the priestly identities of beloved son; chaste spouse; spiritual father; divine physician, and good shepherd could be displayed to express the priestly story of development which a seminarian can aspire to in hope. In addition, local pilgrimages could be arranged to various sites of beauty (parks, museums, hikes, theater). Entertainment, books, movies, art, and pilgrimages can help remold the mind and heart to the image and likeness of God.

Reinforcing and affirming acts of virtue in the seminarian can also lead to the integration of true beauty, and it can be a powerful way to guide these emerging adults to an attitude of gratitude and true freedom of expression. The natural beauty of creation can affectively move their hearts so that experientially, they understand true love and peace. Finally, it is the duty and responsibility of formators to model, teach, advise, exemplify, question, and challenge these young emerging adults in love.

A man of communion formed in the priestly identities of beloved son, chaste spouse, and spiritual father ought to desire to be virtuous and holy in order to please God and direct all things to the service and glory of God. Therefore, the theological virtues are to be evident in candidates who apply for seminary formation and essential for those who commit to candidacy as stated in the promises to the bishop.

The Cardinal Virtues and Formation in the Priestly Identities

Prudence, Justice, Fortitude, and Temperance surround all the other human virtues and, when elevated by grace, guide one into a share of the priestly identities of Christ as Chaste Spouse, Spiritual Father, Spiritual Physician, and Good Shepherd. Through living these virtues, a seminarian will come to know who he is and how he should act in keeping with his relationship, identity, and mission as a diocesan priest.

Prudence

Prudence is 'right reason in action' according to St. Thomas Aquinas and it guides the other virtues by setting rule and measure. It is prudence that immediately guides the judgment of conscience. The prudent man determines and directs his conduct in accordance with this judgment. With the help of this virtue we can apply moral principles to particular cases without error and overcome doubts about the good to achieve and the evil to avoid.[33]

Prudence helps people to organize their lives, acts of intellect, attitudes and actions in order to accomplish the objectives of a contented life in this world. Grace elevates this virtue supernaturally to assist in organizing desires, resources, activities, and behaviors with the goal of being joyful in this life and happy in the eternal life.[34] Prudence helps a priest maintain a balanced approach to life and helps him keep priorities right ordered.

Prudence is an essential virtue for a priest in his identity of Chaste Spouse. It enables the priest to know the good in a given situation and the path for achieving that good. Christ's bride, the Church, looks to her spouse, the priest, to be wise, holy, and prudent. People seek priests for wise counsel in their life's decisions. A priest formed in the identity of Chaste Spouse lives Christ's own spousal love for the Church and can, in the role of Chaste Spouse, love his bride, the Church, back to Christ.

In a survey of seminarian assessments conducted by Archbishop Dolan, he noted that he rarely reads or hears criticisms about doctrinal orthodoxy, devotion to prayer, homiletic ability, or obedience, but often a lack of prudence is cited. Archbishop Dolan gives two examples of a lack of prudence in the newly ordained. In the first example, a vocation director lamented the fact that two young priests left the priesthood soon after ordination: "How could they think their priesthood could survive when they went out six nights a week and did not roll in until after midnight? How could they think their celibacy would survive when they kept exclusive company with attractive women? I worry that some of our young priests are overly confident, almost cocky and do not realize the delicacy of their own vocation. Why are they not more vigilant?"[35] Vigilance and prudence are synonymous.

The second example of a lack of prudence involves not keeping clear and focused goals, which gives life order and meaning. A newly ordained associate asked his pastor which day he would have off, Christmas Eve or Christmas day. The pastor was stunned and asked the priest what he meant. The young priest noted that "I certainly have the right to be with my family on Christmas, so I would expect to be free either Christmas Eve or Day."[36] The hope is that any priest would relish being with his bride, the Church, on Christmas.

How unimaginable it would be for a husband in a marriage to choose to go home to his own family during the holidays, leaving his wife and children.

Observing seminarians in different settings and with different populations can prepare formators how to teach and correct the seminarians to be more prudent, keeping in mind that the best instruction is to be a witness to others in one's own prudent actions and words.

Justice

Justice is the moral virtue that consists in the constant and firm will to give [what is] due to God and neighbor. Justice toward God is called the 'virtue of religion.' Justice toward men disposes one to respect the rights of each and to establish in human relationship the harmony that promotes equity with regard to persons and to the common good. The just man, often mentioned in Sacred Scriptures, is distinguished by habitual right thinking and the uprightness of his conduct toward his neighbor.[37]

All our social relationships are called to be free, total, faithful, and fruitful gifts of self. These qualities are essential for the priestly identity of spiritual fatherhood. Pope Emeritus Benedict XVI reminds us that "Communion always and inseparably has both a vertical and a horizontal sense: it is communion with God and communion with our brothers and sisters. Both dimensions mysteriously converge in the gift of Eucharist."[38] Keeping this in mind, we can understand how anything less than a "free, total, faithful and fruitful gift of self is an act of contraception."[39]

In today's culture, many injustices in the world stem from

the "contraception of the gift of self—a withholding of the gift of our self to God or a preventing of His gift from being received in our heart."[40] Many injustices are a withholding of the gift of our self to our neighbor. The priestly identity of spiritual fatherhood requires laying down one's life for one's neighbor, a total gift of self. In order to receive the love of Father, healing the fear of spousal self-giving and fatherly commitment may be at the heart of human formation.

In seminary formation, a seminarian can have an attitude of having to be right all the time, thus withholding the gift of empathy or understanding. This attitude can cause division among brothers and even isolation on the part of the seminarian if he is closed to opening his own heart to listening to varying opinions. Opinions are not absolute truths and most likely, change over time. "Being right" all the time can cut off the fruit of conversion individually and communally. Spiritual fatherhood bears fruit in the conversion of others and their growth in holiness. The priestly identity of spiritual father requires faithfulness and justice to all, and prayer is essential to living out this call.

Formators can help seminarians assess their own virtue of justice and ability to be spiritual fathers by having them ask themselves these questions: How often do I cut corners in my work? Sidestep my duties? Cheat others of what I owe them, even in small things (including my bishop and people of the diocese who pay for my education in seminary)? How often do I spend time in virtual reality, rather than developing personal relationships? If a seminarian can answer, "Frequently" to any of the previous questions, then the virtue of justice is not deeply rooted in his character; "no one can keep his self-respect unless he is first just towards others."[41]

Fortitude

Fortitude is the moral virtue that ensures firmness in difficulties and constancy in the pursuit of the good. It strengthens the resolve to resist temptations and to overcome obstacles in the moral life. The virtue of fortitude enables one to conquer fear, even fear of death, and to face trials and persecutions. It disposes one even to renounce and sacrifice his life in defense of a just cause.[42]

A sign of a culture's decline is the "absence of admiration for people of courage."[43] Since many countries' current world view is one of individualism, the natural virtue of courage has been reduced to "selfism." In other terms, why would one want to risk losing his own life for another when it would mean giving up that which is more important (i.e., personal fulfillment or pleasures)?

In contrast to the culture's self-centered goal of courage, which can be described as bravado or foolhardiness, courage as a Christian virtue enables a person to confront danger and endure difficulty to achieve the ultimate goal of salvation or help others achieve the same goal. Fortitude, by this defini-tion, is one of the seven gifts of the Holy Spirit and through the Holy Spirit empowers a person to suffer with those who suffer, and to mourn with those who mourn, and to pick up one's cross and carry it. Is this description not congruent with the identity of spiritual physician?

The spiritual physician must live Christ's own healing mission of love to His bride, the Church. Being a spiritual physician requires the virtue of fortitude in order to: provide good counsel, give just absolution in the Sacrament of Pen-ance, speak the truth in love through daily preaching, deliver wise spiritual direction, administer the Sacrament of the Sick, and be merciful in daily encounters with all whom he meets. The spiritual physician receives the supernatural grace of the virtue of fortitude in his ability to hold the sins of others confidential. The supernatural virtue can also elevate the spiritual physician's ability to be compassionate and forgiving, even when confronted with unthinkable depravities through sin.

Temperance

Temperance is the moral virtue that moderates the attraction of pleasures and provides balance in the use of created goods. It ensures the will's mastery over instincts and keeps desires within the limits of what is honorable. The temperate person directs the sensitive appetites toward what is good and maintains a healthy discretion.[44]

The virtue of temperance "ensures the will's mastery over instincts and keeps desires within the limits of what is honorable."[45] In other words, the virtue of temperance, along with all the virtues, forms the priestly identity of good shepherd by allowing the priest to live Christ's servant-love (i.e., by continually seeking to serve others rather than demanding to be served by them). The priestly identity of good shepherd is part of a call to priesthood, "not a career; a redefinition of self, not just a new ministry, a way of life, not a job; a state of being, not just a function; a permanent lifelong commitment, not a temporary style of service; an identity, not just a role."[46] Temperance is a guide to know how to use the attractive things of life in a way that contributes to one's natural goals while keeping the priest faithful to his identity of good shepherd. Morally, this virtue directs men to understand that all pleasurable things in life must be directed toward their salvation and the salvation of others.

Formators can determine if a seminarian is being formed in the priestly identity of good shepherd by assessing if he is happy in life. In other words, is he manifesting heartfelt joy in his life? Unhappiness can lead to intemperance and suffering. In many cases, an attempt to relieve this suffering can lead to unhealthy behaviors that can become compulsive and even addictive.

The degree to which a seminarian embraces his commitment to celibacy in seminary "is critical to how happy he will be as a priest," according to a recent psychological study on *Why Priests are Happy*, by Stephen Rossetti.[47] If he is unhappy as a chaste seminarian, he will surely be unhappy as a celibate and chaste priest and unable to fulfill his priestly identity of good shepherd.

Conclusion: The Call to Communion

A man of communion is someone "who makes a gift of himself and is able to receive the gift of others."[48] This character development can be achieved only through "the love of God and service to others."[49] Such a person must be more than a man of example; by continually living out of the love of Christ, he will be a man reoriented and conformed to Christ.

Ordination to priesthood is not about the development of one's own powers and gifts; it is a sacrament which means: "I give what I myself cannot give; I do something that is not my work; I am on a mission and have become the bearer of that which another has committed to my charge."[50] Therefore, no one can declare himself a priest for a community by his own "fiat." This gift of priesthood can be received only from the Sacrament of Holy Orders by "entering into the mission that makes me the messenger and instrument of another."[51] This disposition of selflessness is essential to the "priestly ministry that can lead to authentic human affective maturity and fulfillment."[52]

Bodily comfort and material security can take humanity only so far. The human spirit of man can be satisfied only by the Father who created us, the Son who redeemed us, and the Spirit who is love and abides in us. Now, more than ever, men who enter seminary formation must be taught and witnessed to by formators and spiritual directors so they, too, can become the light of Christ that will bear truth to the darkness in this world.

Who can better understand today's culture of darkness than those emerging adults who have been called by God out of the darkness of society into the light? For this reason, it is the hope of this psychologist and author that rectors of all seminaries will be encouraged to hire staff psychologists (who, themselves, live virtuous lives) to help formators become "foster parents" to seminarians, as Joseph and Mary did with Jesus in Nazareth. What a sacred mission it is for rectors, spiritual directors, formators, faculty, and psychologists to be commissioned by God to form the future *men of communion*.

BENCHMARKS FOR A MAN OF COMMUNION

THEOLOGICAL VIRTUES

Is a man ready to be accepted into seminary formation?
(*Is his true desire to move away from the secular pop culture and toward God?*)
VIRTUE OF FAITH-"*man freely commits his entire self to God.*"

Entrance Criteria 1: "There need be evidence that they should commit themselves wholeheartedly to carrying out that discernment."[53]

Measurement for the Virtue of Faith

1. Commitment to prayer (daily holy hour).
2. Willingness to have an undivided heart (live chastity of the heart–free from world's distractions) measured by willingness to keep commitment to discern priestly vocation without engaging in external relationships that lead to emotional or physical bonding.
3. Be open and able to freely receive direction and formation through obedience to authority.

VIRTUE OF HOPE– *"desire the kingdom of heaven and eternal life as our happiness, placing our trust in Christ's promises and relying not on our own strength, but on the help of the grace of the Holy Spirit."*
Entrance Criteria 2: "Evidence that God brought them to the seminary to discern whether or not they are really called to priesthood."[54]

Measurement for the Virtue of Hope

1. Disposition of the heart by an attitude of receptivity;
   a. Is it an attitude of *compliance* (choosing acts based on external rewards or punishments–to live in a state of compliance is exhausting and incongruent with one's own inner meanings)?
   b. Is it an attitude of *identification* (choosing acts based on specific expectations within a relationship–a lack of freedom to be true to one's own internal beliefs)?
   c. Is it an attitude of *integration* (internal choices based

on a personal value system–living an integrated life is energizing since it is in harmony with one's own internal values and deepest convictions)?

2. Are they willing to rely on God's grace?

a. To trust that God is in control of their lives through their formators so that they can overcome unhealthy compulsive behaviors that they recognize in themselves as they come to a deeper knowledge of themselves through their intellectual, human, pastoral and spiritual pillars of formation?

VIRTUE OF CHARITY–"*love God above all things for his own sake, and our neighbor as ourselves for the love of God.*"[55]
Entrance Criteria 3: "And a growing sense of confirmation of that call." [56]

Measurement for the Virtue of Love

1. Does the seminarian embrace the identity of beloved son and brother as the core foundation for all the priestly identities?

a. A beloved son has trust, confidence, and a deep peace that he can depend upon those who care for him because he trusts completely in the Heavenly Father that he is loved for who he is. A beloved brother learns how to choose friends and remain loyal and steadfast with a friend in difficulty. These foundational identities, especially that of beloved son, are deeply rooted in the identity of Jesus as the Beloved Son of the Father.

i. "It is the Father who reveals to us who we really are; so we must be fathered into our true identity, which means being fathered by God."[57]

ii. Once the identity of beloved son is

received, he can become a loyal brother to others, making a deliberate commitment to go beyond the normal likes and dislikes that are prompted by clashing personalities and attitudes.

iii. In addition, a beloved brother can communicate with his peers in clarity and charity. He understands that opinions are not absolute truths and can change over time, thus letting go of his need to be "right" in every discussion or argument. These skills must be taught, practiced, and measured in growth by formation.

CARDINAL VIRTUES
Is a man ready to receive Candidacy (Theology I)?

Prudence, Justice, Fortitude, and Temperance surround all the other human virtues and, when elevated by grace, they become the moral virtues.

VIRTUE OF PRUDENCE—*human virtue prudence helps people to organize their lives and actions in order to accomplish the objectives of a contented life in this world.*

1. Is there orderliness in his life?
    a. *Physically*—living and hygiene orderliness; good "physical health."[58]
    b. *Humanly*—overall time management and being able to set proper boundaries with self and others; "A balanced lifestyle and balance in making judgments"[59]; "'good' mental health."[60]
    c. *Intellectually*—procrastination disproportions.
    d. *Pastorally*—effectiveness of use of time, a filial receptivity of joy and obedience to the pastor in charge.
    e. *Spiritually*—prayer life is the first priority in his life.

VIRTUE OF JUSTICE—*justice demands honesty and fairness in relationship with others. The natural virtue of religion calls us to honor God and observe the natural law while maintaining certain standards of good behavior.*

1. Honesty and fairness in his relationships with self, others, and God.

    a. *Physically (socially)*—do they have healthy, long-lasting friendships, and do those relationships bring them closer to God or away from God?

    b. *Humanly*—do they have insight and take responsibility for their actions, and are they open and honest in the evaluation process and to their vocation director?

    c. *Intellectually*—have they integrated knowledge wisely, and are they honest in their dedication to studies? Do they share the intellectual gifts they have been given with their brothers?

    d. *Pastorally*—are they open to receive constructive feedback in their apostolics and apply that feedback with openness and joy? Are they open to others' opinions (if they disagree) without judging the person?

    e. *Spiritually*—are they open and honest with God through spiritual direction (aware)?

VIRTUE OF FORTITUDE—*Fortitude enables a person to confront danger and endure difficulty to achieve the ultimate goal of salvation or to help others achieve the same goal. Fortitude by this definition is one of the seven gifts of the Holy Spirit and through the Holy Spirit empowers a person to suffer with those who suffer, and to mourn with those who mourn, and to pick up one's cross and carry it.*

1. Is the man willing to suffer with and for the kingdom of God? This means pushing against fear by picking up one's cross and following Christ.

    a. *Physically*–self-mastery of body by pushing against the fear of poor body image. Removing all obstacles in one's life that may take him from this goal (e.g., food; smoking; over-exercise; overemphasis on sports, inappropriate relationships).

    b. *Humanly*–are they integrated interiorly and externally affectively and effectively? In other words, can they push against the fear of loneliness and not give in to temptations?

    c. *Intellectually*–can they distinguish between the world's notion of courage (bravado) and the supernatural virtue of fortitude and be a witness of fortitude, if called?

    d. *Pastorally*–do they have the capacity to push against the fear of not getting what they want (selfish needs–i.e., time, social media, etc.) and be empathic to the needs and sufferings of others by responding to them in a timely manner?

    e. *Spiritually*–are they rooted in a balanced life of prayer? Can they push against their own rigidity by having the courage and fortitude to die to self in areas to which they may be inordinately attached, such as liturgical practices or aesthetic practices, and always seek permission of spiritual director?

VIRTUE OF TEMPERANCE–*is a guide to help us use the attractive things of life in a way that contributes to our natural goals in life. It also involves taking care of our own legitimate needs and maintaining balance in one's life. Morally, this virtue directs us to understand that all pleasurable things in life must be directed toward our salvation and the salvation of others.*

1. A good assessment of this virtue is to determine the

happiness in the seminarians' lives.

Physically; Humanly; Pastorally; Intellectually and Spiritually

a. Are they free of, or nearly free of, any unhealthy compulsive or addictive behavior?

b. Can they commit to a life of chastity and live it out in seminary on a daily basis?

c. Do they have "self-mastery and self-discipline?"[61]

The PPF requires chaste living three years before ordination.

VIRTUES AND PRIESTLY IDENTITIES

Is a Man Ready for Ordination to Transitional Deacon?

An authentic benchmark for the transitional deacon is for him to understand that *faith which sees the love of God revealed in the pierced heart of Jesus on the Cross gives rise to love.* By the overshadowing of the Holy Spirit, the Lord descends upon the ordained deacon to give the deacon His heart (that is, the "Sacred Heart of Jesus"). Love is possible when we are able to practice it knowing (self-knowledge) we are created in the image of God as beloved children of the Father. The diaconal candidate ought to interiorly, through his own prayer life and witness, have integrated the belief that love is the light—and, in the end, the only light—that can always illuminate a world grown dim. This awareness gives him and his bride, the Church, the courage needed to keep promoting a culture of life while continuing to live and work in the current culture of death.

The diaconal candidate ought to understand responsible freedom. Responsible freedom is not just spontaneity of movement and physical response but it is his ability to recognize the implications of all his decisions. It is a willingness to carry the consequences of all his choices. It requires an accountability that understands his sexuality as a personal gift and responsibility?[62] When self-awareness and responsible freedom converge, creativity occurs and new life can begin.

The diaconal candidate ought to have a disposition of interior silence. Living a virtuous life can help form a man to desire silence both exteriorly and interiorly even in the midst of the daily distractions of life. Exterior silence preserves the purpose of interior silence since interior silence prepares a man to receive and remain in communion with God. Silence ordered toward communion with God is essential for a priest to live a joyful and happy life.

As the diaconal candidate's life grows in intimacy with the Trinity and Mary, all the virtues will be ignited so that he can lead a virtuous life as a priest, and ultimately become a saint. From this intimate communion, the priestly identities which have been stirring in the diaconal candidate's heart will lead him to his mission as a diocesan priest.

TRANSITIONAL DIACONATE BENCHMARKS:

1. Does the seminarian preparing for transitional deacon have self-knowledge and self-awareness?

2. Does the seminarian preparing for transitional Deacon have a disposition of interior silence?

3. Interiorly through his own prayer life and witness, has he integrated the belief that love is the light—and in the end, the only light?

4. Does the diaconal candidate understand responsible freedom?

   a. Responsible freedom is not just spontaneity of

movement and physical response but responsibility is his ability to recognize the implications of all his decisions. It is a willingness to carry the consequences of all his choices.

    b. In addition, does he understand his sexuality as a personal gift and responsibility?[63]

    5. When self-awareness and responsible freedom converge, creativity occurs. Creativity becomes generative if it is from our inner being as a human person. Does the diaconal candidate have the ability to participate in making new life? (Pastoral assignments).

    6. Does the diaconal candidate's life embrace all the theological virtues and does he have a spiritual disposition to practice and live all the natural virtues and have all doubts removed concerning Church teaching?

    7. Does the diaconal candidate have a deepening capacity for intimacy and the confidence to appropriately self-disclose in the gift of mutual sharing, first with the Lord, then friends?

    8. Does he have the ability to relate (connect physically, emotionally, and spiritually) and the "skills for leadership and collaboration with women and men?"[64]

    9. The transitional deacon's evident integration of the priestly identities of beloved son, brother, spouse, and father can be clear measurable benchmarks for advancing to ordination.

NOTES

1. David Kerr, *Pope Challenges US Bishops to Revive Christian Culture* (Vatican City: Catholic News Agency, June 5, 2012). http://www.catholicnewsagency.com/news/pope-challenges-us-bishops-to-revive-christian-culture/.

2. Benedict Groeschel, *The Virtue Driven Life.* (Huntington, IN: Our Sunday Visitor, 2006).

3. Entrance into seminary, Candidacy [Theology I], and Pre-Deaconate [Theology III].

4. David Kerr, *Pope Challenges US Bishops to Revive Christian Culture* (Vatican City: Catholic News Agency, June 5, 2012). http://www.catholicnewsagency.com/news/pope-challenges-us-bishops-to-revive-christian-culture/.

5. George Barna, *Futurecast: What Today's Trends Mean for Tomorrow's World* (Austin, Texas: Tyndale Publishing, 2011).

6. Christian Smith, *Lost in Transition: The Dark Side of Emerging Adulthood* (New York: Oxford University Press, 2011), 12.

7. Ibid.

8. Sara Konrath, *Empathy: College Students Don't Have as Much as They Used To* (Ann Arbor, MI: University of Michigan, May 27, 2010). http://ns.umich.edu/new/releases/7724-empathy-college-students-don-t-have-as-much-as-they-used-to.

9. Ibid.

10. Ibid.

11. Smith, 9.

12. Ibid.

13. Ibid., 152.

14. Ibid., 10.

15. Ibid., 229.

16. *Catechism of the Catholic Church (CCC)* (Washington, DC: USCCB Publishing, 2000), sec. 1803.

17. Ibid.

18. *Catechism of the Catholic Church*, sec. 1803, citing St. Gregory of Nyssa, *De beatitudinibus*, 1:PG 44, 1200D.

19. *Catechism of the Catholic Church*, 1548. In the ecclesial service of the ordained minister, it is Christ himself who is present to his Church as Head of his Body, Shepherd of his flock, high priest of the redemptive sacrifice, Teacher of Truth. This is what the Church means by saying that the priest, by virtue of the sacrament of Holy Orders, acts *in persona Christi Capitis.*

20. *Catechism of the Catholic Church*, secs. 1834, 1804.

21. Dietrich Von Hildebrand, *Christian Ethics* (New York: McKay, 1953).

22. Rudolf Allers, *Forming Character in Adolescents* (Fort Collins, CO: Roman Catholic Books, 1940), 119.

23. If a person has a fragmented sense of self, too strong a focus on virtue maybe unfruitful and, therefore, the person ought not be in seminary. The theory and practice of virtue remain valid and true, but something additional is needed for this man and ought to be taken care of outside seminary formation. Greg Kolodziejczak, in private conversation with the author, 2013.

24. *Catechism of the Catholic Church*, sec. 1804.

25. Gregory J. Schlesselmann, *The Seminary Rector: Forming Priests in Nazareth* (Omaha, NE: The Institute for Priestly Formation, 2012), 16.

26. Groeschel.

27. Archbishop Timothy Dolan, *Priests for the Third Millennium* (Huntington, IN: Our Sunday Visitor, Inc, 2000.), 21-22.

28. Ibid., 20.

29. Ibid.

30. Ibid., 43; Blessed John Paul II, *Pastores Dabo Vobis* (1992), sec. 22.

31. Edward Garesche, SJ, *The Catholic Book of Character and Success* (Manchester, NH: Sophia Institute Press, 2003), 14.

32. Ibid., 20.

33. *Catechism of the Catholic Church*, sec. 1806.

34. Groeschel.

35. Dolan, 122.

36. Ibid., 123.

37. *Catechism of the Catholic Church*, sec. 1807.

38. JV Johnston, *The Need for a New Witness* (St. Louis Prayer Breakfast, May 24, 2012).

39. Ibid.

40. Pope Emeritus Benedict XVI, *Sacramentum Caritatis* (2007), sec. 76.

41. Garesche, 14.

42. *Catechism of the Catholic Church*, sec. 1808.

43. Groeschel, 68.

44. *Catechism of the Catholic Church*, sec. 1809.

45. Ibid.

46. Dolan, 228.

47. Stephen J. Rossetti, *Why Priests are Happy: A Study of the Psychological and Spiritual Health of Priests* (Notre Dame, IN: Ave Maria Press, 2011), 105.

48. United States Conference of Catholic Bishops, *Program of Priestly Formation*, 5th ed. (PPF) (Washington, DC: USCCB, 2006), sec. 115.

49. Ibid., sec. 74.

50. Joseph Cardinal Ratzinger, *Called to Communion* (SFO, CA: Ignatius Press, 1996), 115.

51. Ibid., 115.

52. Ibid.

53. *Program of Priestly Formation*, sec. 22.
54. Ibid.
55. *Catechism of the Catholic Church*, sec. 1822.
56. *Program of Priestly Formation*, sec. 22.
57. Schlesselmann, 25.
58. *Program of Priestly Formation*, sec. 280.
59. Ibid.
60. Ibid.
61. Ibid.
62. *Pastores Dabo Vobis*, secs. 43-44; 87.
63. Ibid.
64. *Program of Priestly Formation*, sec. 280.

THE RELATIONAL CAPACITY OF FUTURE PRIESTS

FR. WALTER OXLEY

Introduction

Priestly formation today is taking a greater turn toward forming men of communion at both the affective and spiritual level in order that they become adequately prepared to minister to God's holy people. This goal may be conceptualized and understood under the hermeneutic of the intelligence of the heart.[1] The scope of this paper is to examine the import of these realities within the context of the spiritual and human formation of seminarians. In order to accomplish this objective, it is necessary to address how affective maturity is understood within the five identities of the priest and to see how it contributes to the priest becoming a man of communion.[2] Only in the rediscovery of the heart as the spiritual center of the seminarian and the discovery of the value of affectivity, therein, are we able to truly discover the relational capacity of any one seminarian.

The Heart

The term *heart*, as used in both the Old and the New Testaments, is applied in a primary sense to the whole person, the totality of the human person, and the interior man.[3] Biblical passages indicate that the heart is the spiritual center of the person, the place where affectivity, thought, and freedom have their origin. The heart, thus, symbolizes what is both deepest and most personally intimate in man. As it is the place where the "I" dwells, the heart becomes the place of personal subjectivity, unique individuality, interpersonal encounter, and communion with the "thou" of the other.[4]

Put simply, the biblical understanding of the heart must be fully accepted as a viable anthropological and theological reality in order for the realm of affectivity to be fully valued as a necessary component of personal holiness.[5] In the heart, a man becomes attuned to noticing the sensations, movements, thoughts, and desires therein. By relying simply on the development of intellect and will, we will not have an adequate understanding of the authentic personhood to which the seminarian is called.[6]

State of the Seminary in the United States

The culture of seminaries throughout the United States of America today is, in large part, a culture of doctrinal fidelity to Catholic teaching. Fidelity to the teaching of the Church in areas of faith and morals, which, of course, includes fidelity to the Church's teaching on the ordained priesthood, enables the seminarian to trust and, therefore, confide in the priest faculty of the seminary, both in the external as well as the internal forum. The seminarians of the third millennium have high expectations for the priest faculty. The reality that these expectations are largely being met places the seminary in an advantageous position to address the next phase of seminary formation: the development of the intelligence of the heart.

Since there is now present within diocesan seminaries a near universal orthodoxy, the seminarian is now offered conditions with which to grow in his capacity to relate more capably to both God and his neighbor. During the years of the battle for doctrinal fidelity within the seminary, the role of the heart was often held in suspicion by seminarians who longed for required doctrinal fidelity, often seemingly absent, and to which all of their energy for recovery was directed. Furthermore, the heart was often regarded not only as unnecessary, but negative, as it was often reduced to mere emotion and sentimentality. In the seminarian's mind, both emotion and sentiment were judged to be the most significant contributing factors for the problem of infidelity in both doctrine and practice.

In order for the seminarian to be formed in living out the priestly identities (Beloved Son, Chaste Spouse, Spiritual Father, Spiritual Physician, and Good Shepherd), he must have an openness to be formed in ways that include much more than doctrinal fidelity. The pastoral skills required here are necessarily built upon a human foundation that includes affective maturity, self-awareness, self-knowledge, and self-gift.[7]

Without the affective spiritual transformation of the formator, his words will be only words, and he will not recognize any generativity in his ministry for the seminarians. Through his own witness of contemplation, even in action, the priest formator is, thus, able to be a sign of the relational capacity with both God and neighbor that the Church desires for her future priests.

The priest formator is invited to accept the coming of Christ within his own heart, through his own embrace of suffering and transformation, so that he may become a credible sign of invitation to the seminarian to desire the five priestly identities. The priest formator, thus, must be much more than a mere academician or administrator as he is invited each day to be engaged in his own personal contemplative journey with Jesus Christ in order that he may possess the gift of priesthood and, thus, be capable of sharing that gift with the seminarian.

Beloved Son and Spiritual Father

In order to become a chaste spouse and spiritual father, a young man must first become a loving son and a loving brother.[8] If a seminarian expects that he may become a spiritual father without first becoming a son or a brother, he is very much mistaken. He may, however, be influenced to think he can become a spiritual father if relationality and affective maturity are dismissed in favor of fatherhood as an impersonal role demonstrating skill sets. He may be inclined to dismiss affectivity for two reasons: 1) the absence of a loving father in his childhood or early adulthood, or he may have been influenced by 2) an overbearing and demanding fatherly presence where his biological father lacked the necessary affective components of the presence of love in fatherhood.

Those seminarians in the first category will often try to compensate for their lack of being loved by a father by actually becoming the father they never had. While often laudable, this tendency can also have significant drawbacks.

The challenge for this type of seminarian is that he has never encountered true fatherhood, never experienced fatherhood at the critical phases of his own human development. This deficiency can be catastrophic because the living out of fatherhood is based merely on a concept of what it should be. In this seminarian, there may be problems of neediness, and even co-dependency, that accompany his attempt to live fatherhood.

A seminarian who has experienced a strict, demanding, and perhaps even verbally or emotionally abusive father during his childhood years also may have the desire to live fatherhood as a priest. If such a seminarian has not acknowledged and related his experience of having this type of biological father to his Father in heaven, this seminarian will have a deficient and default image of how the Heavenly Father actually relates to him. If this experience is not acknowledged, related to God in prayer, and healed, this seminarian will also have an understanding of spiritual fatherhood that reflects a misrepresentation of the Fatherhood of God.

Because of his built-in default image of God the Father as the rule-giver and the demander of perfection, the seminarian aspires to this kind of fatherhood. He may come to identify himself primarily as the source of authority for his parish, the giver of the law. His identity is, henceforth, formed around how obedient his parishioners are to his authority. If his authority is not acknowledged and he does not receive the proper homage that he believes is owed to him by his office (this, of course, understood distinctly from the obedience of faith to which all Catholics are called), he may become angry and combative[9] because such a response is the only kind that he understands, primarily because it was the response that was modeled for him in his youth.[10] It may be that the seminarian understands fatherhood solely as his being the transmitter of the doctrine and the law of the Church. This transmission, however, while absolutely essential to the vocation of the priest as spiritual father, does not completely define fatherhood.

The seminary formator must, therefore, take heed in formation against any tendency in seminarians to raise their voices in an angry manner during preaching, becoming curt, impolite, or dismissive when the needs of people are presented to him.[11]

This type of seminarian may understand himself to be very important and a model for following the moral law, but those in his parish either chuckle or are saddened by the brokenness within him that he fails to acknowledge. They begin to regard him more and more as irrelevant and isolated because of his lack of capacity to relate to them in their own struggle to live the Christian life in the world.[12] The priest may even become very proud of himself for his accomplishments (narcissism), which matter little to the lay faithful whom he is called to minister.

This incapacity to relate to the real world concerns of parishioners within his parish, particularly middle-aged biological fathers, may lead the future priest to default to the comfortable surroundings of his past seminary experience. This may be manifested by his emotional distance from parishioners as he reverts to a more scholarly approach to pastoral ministry. With the embrace of this more distant identity and his incapacity to both relate and communicate, he becomes the parish priest only for the few who appreciate his idiosyncrasies.[13] He begins to talk more than listen and begins to rely more upon superficial social experiences that have no relevance or purpose in bringing the people into a relationship with the Holy Trinity.[14] The priest also may begin to cling to power and take psychological consolation only in the office that he has been given because he lacks the lived experience of being loved by God and by the people whom he is called to serve.

Often, at the root of this problem and, perhaps, occasionally unheeded by the seminarian himself as a place in need of healing are the problems of scrupulosity and perfectionism. The reform-minded seminarian who lacks the affective maturity of the heart is the most likely candidate to bear these struggles. The priest faculty must be aware that bearing these psychological struggles in the context of priestly ministry can become a great burden for the parish community–and even for the priest himself.[15] . While these characteristics often do not manifest themselves very well in the seminary as problems (as the seminarian often excels in the academic and rule-of-life expectations of the seminary), they quickly become problems in the context of parish life. One finds that the priest is neither formed nor capable of practicing the "Gospel Discernment" required for pastoral ministry in a world where both the wheat and the weeds "co-exist,"[16] nor is he capable of relating to others within his parish as a brother and a father.

Chaste Spouse

Young couples seeking marriage and married couples who are looking for continued direction in living fidelity, love, and openness to life together need to find a pastor who is both affectively mature and capable of understanding human love.

How often we hear, and are convinced, by the lie that priests are not capable of relating to married couples! If a priest is living out of the depths of his celibacy, he actually becomes an expert on human love. He understands that human love is much deeper than the genital expression of the reality, and he is able to lead both the men and the women into a deeper awareness of the essential role of sacrifice that is spousal love.

To be a chaste spouse to the Church and to mirror in his own love for the Church a sign that is credible and appealing to the husband in his love for his wife, the future priest must first understand what it means to experience human love. If the seminarian has no lived experience of being loved, then he has lived only out of his intellect during his life and has either suppressed the reality of the heart, or, perhaps, he does not understand that there is such a place within him.[17] Without affective maturity, his love for the Church will lack the necessary human dimensions of the experience of love.

The typical seminarian, who is now more often young and chaste upon his arrival in the seminary, will, therefore, need much growth in the area of psycho-sexual maturity before he is actually able to minister to people. If he does not grow in his psycho-sexual identity, he will not be able to adequately minister from and out of his celibacy because his celibacy has not been received as a sacrifice. Furthermore, if his sexual desire is suppressed, a default image of the woman may emerge based upon his own personal fear, as opposed to a woman being understood as complementary and valued for her "feminine genius."[18] Women intuitively know, because of the manner in which he relates to them, when a priest is not able to give them spiritual direction or counsel. When a future priest either does not appreciate, or does not understand, the feminine genius, then he is truly not capable of fully entering into the fullness of pastoral ministry.

There also is a second possibility that the seminarian experienced in his life the various pseudo-loves that are falsely identified as real love. The pseudo-loves are in the form of Internet pornography and the sexual promiscuity of the culture that pervades the *ethos* of high school and college campuses. This seminarian will then need much inner healing before he may begin to adequately understand, appreciate, relate, and receive the great value of femininity.

The capacity of the priest for a chaste receptivity of the feminine, with the appropriate and necessary boundaries, gives the priest the freedom to engage in dynamic ministry for all the faithful. The freedom may take years to attain becauseof his prior engagement in the hyper-sexualized society in which we live. Upon his decision to live a life of chastity, the seminarian will most likely, for a number of years, remain ambivalent about its goodness. Once he is free from any second thoughts regarding his chaste vocation, his priesthood becomes enriched, deepened, and much more contemplative.

The future priest is then called to embrace the Church as his Bride as he becomes married to the Church at his priestly ordination. He is called to love her like he would have loved his own wife and, thus, love every person within the Church as part of the body of his bride. Each and every individual woman is not his bride but makes up part of his bride; thus, he does not claim any one woman within the Church as his spouse but only the people as a corporate whole. This relationship requires him to have both the freedom and the virtue to be able to relate with women both young and old while, at the same time, being utterly detached from each and every woman whom he is called to serve.

Subsequently, no woman may rightfully claim the priest as her own since he is in the person of Jesus Christ as Head of the Church. She may want to cling to the priest, as in the case of Mary Magdalene with Jesus, seeing the qualities that she desires in a man, but never finding those desires met in the life of her own personal vocation. If a priest is an integrated man, he will be attractive to the holy woman, and the holy woman must take great caution so that her desires are, therefore, properly ordered not to the priest, but only to Jesus, as the priest is in Jesus with the Father, and his heart is already totally claimed. Mary is able to protect this celibate exclusivity that the priest must maintain. The celibate exclusivity of the priest certainly will come with the "sting" and sacrifice of celibacy,[19] but it is from that sacrifice that the abundance of a dynamic ministry both springs forth from the life of the priest himself and becomes appealing to those who truly know human love.

Good Shepherd

To lead, the future priest must first understand and experience how to be led. Because of unaddressed father wounds, the future priest may find himself to have significant problems with authority, most noticeably in his relationship with his bishop. A priest may have unreasonable expectations for his bishop or an image of perfection that will never be able to be met. He may desire more affirmation or praise for his efforts and accomplishments, and he is always left wanting because he does not find his need for affirmation met by his bishop. Furthermore, he may form opinions that his bishop is not courageous enough, traditional enough, decisive enough, overly dialogical, too compromising, etc. The list could continue *ad infinitum*. He may feel that his rights as a priest have been infringed upon by the college of bishops, and so he has adopted a defensive posture to protect himself and his rights from their perceived unjust or political actions.

The priest must be affectively and spiritually prepared to shepherd his people in communion with his local bishop. If he is not able to do this, there is a significant deficiency both in his own exercise of the priestly ministry and in the parish that he has been asked to lead, sanctify, and govern on behalf of the bishop. Therefore, seminary formators must take vigilance to address early warning signs of negative affective tendencies of a seminarian in relationship to his bishop, and also to the body of bishops as a whole in the United States. When the seminarian envisions himself as a priest who is the equal of his bishop, he is narcissistic, or intellectually elite, and has evidently not properly grown in the virtue of humility that needs to be present in a high degree, insofar as he is called to understand his bishop as the pre-eminent and superior teacher in the diocese.[20] Without accepting the development in doctrine on the theology of the bishop in the relationship to the priest in the Dogmatic Constitution on the Church of the Second Vatican Council,[21] the priest will never be able to theologically live out the identity of the Good Shepherd according the mind of the Church for the priest.

Spiritual Physician

The priest is called to embrace the priestly identity of spiritual physician. In order for this to occur, the priest must have the human freedom and maturity to be able to be open and docile enough to receive the gifts of the Holy Spirit that are necessary for him to bring about spiritual healing within the faithful who are in need of such. The priest is called to be receptive and open to the spiritual healing that a penitent may need, beginning in the confessional. Here, in the context of the Sacrament of Penance, a priest is an instrument for spiritual healing and can bring the penitent to an understanding of sin's source, or root, as often the sinful acts are done as a result of a deeper wound which has been unaddressed or even remains unknown for many years.[22] These core wounds may bind the penitent spiritually. A confessor who is a spiritual physician is capable of helping the penitent listen for the causes of his or her actual sins within his or her wounded heart. When the root of the sin is named, the penitent can lift these wounds up for healing, as well.

For the seminarian to become a spiritual physician, he must be well trained, at minimum, in the first set of rules of St. Ignatius of Loyola for the Discernment of Spirits. Particular attention should be given here to the 13th Rule of St. Ignatius, wherein the classical spiritual teacher, St. Ignatius, teaches how the evil spirit is bound by the act of making his tactics known through transparency.[23] The seminarian himself must develop a habit of transparency, particularly with his relationship with his spiritual director within the internal forum. Without transparency, the seminarian has no potential whatsoever to become an instrument for deliverance[24] and spiritual healing.

Without transparency, the seminarian will certainly be capable and fortified with the spiritual power and capacity for sacramental absolution after ordination, but nothing further. One can become a good confessor while, at the same time,

not be a spiritual physician. A good confessor is prepared
only intellectually for his celebration of the Sacrament of
Penance. He is intellectually prepared through his knowledge
of Catholic moral teaching and Canon Law. However, the
intellectual preparation is actually the minimum. One must
ask: were St. John Vianney and St. Padre Pio satisfied with
the transmission of faithful and accurate moral teaching,
in form of counsel and penance alone, in their celebration
of the Sacrament of Penance? Why were their confessional
lines so long? What was the "more" that these confessors
were offering the penitents in the confessional? Was not their
transparency to the spiritual gifts overflowing in the form
of the "doctoring" that they were exercising? The Catholic
faithful are often looking for something more in their celebration of the Sacrament of Penance. In the parish, the Catholic
faithful who are actively praying are often seeking confessors
who are capable of acting as a spiritual physician, and, thus,
subsequently as a spiritual director outside of the Sacrament
of Penance.

Because of the climate in the Church as a result of the
scourge of the sexual abuse of minors by priests, some
priests have become very concerned with the possibility of
a false accusation, or of becoming vulnerable to legal action
being brought against them for simply dutifully exercising
their priestly duties. Priests ordained in the last decades, and
even some seminarians, are rightfully wounded by the sins of
their brother priests and how those sins have affected the lay
faithful. Due to this fear, which often challenges the desire of
the priest to want to control his environment, the priest will
all too often want to default to measures to protect himself
within the ministry of the Sacrament of Penance, as opposed

to becoming more of a spiritual physician.

Manifestations of this fear are found in the priest confessor seeking first to exercise his canonical right not to celebrate the Sacrament of Penance in the "face-to- face" format, but to require in all circumstances the anonymous format in order to protect himself from a potential accusation. The difficulty with this growing tendency is not so much in that the doctoring of the soul cannot occur in the anonymous format but that the disposition of the priest becomes more focused on the protection of his own person from harm than it does on doctoring the soul of the penitent. It is imperative for the seminarian to understand that the priestly ministry he exercises in the person of Jesus Christ is in the hands of the Father for its protection, and while he certainly should be prepared to be vigilant and prudent as a future priest in protecting both himself and the Church from a false accusation, he does not want to minister out of fear.

Seminary formators must continue to promote and foster healthy relationships of mutual trust between the seminarian, his bishop, and, in turn, the lay faithful whom the seminarian will soon serve. A healthy and filial relationship of the seminarian with his bishop will certainly assist him in not succumbing to fear, rather cling to the fact that his bishop will see any situation through with due justice, concern, and fairness for both priest and people.

Conclusion

We live in a time within the Church where the gifts of the Holy Spirit have the potential to overflow in the life of the priest for the building up of the Church. After a period of much trial, both in terms of doctrinal fidelity and in the continual purification of the Church in the wake of the priestly scandals, the priest is able to emerge as humble, purified, and dependent upon the great gifts of God, as opposed to his own talents and power. Only with humility will the Father truly be able to raise the priest to the level that he desires for the sake of the New Evangelization. The Father creates the Beloved Son, the Spiritual Father, the Good Shepherd, the Chaste Spouse, and the Spiritual Physician, with much cooperation on the part of the seminarian, insofar as he has the desire to be created anew for the glory of God. New and dynamic forms of priestly ministry await us, with a new outpouring of the Holy Spirit upon the future priests of the United States, for the New Evangelization.[25]

NOTES

1. Blessed John Paul II, *Pastores Dabo Vobis* (1992), sec. 43. See also *Pastores Dabo Vobis*, sec. 51 "To be pastorally effective, intellectual formation is to be integrated with a spirituality marked by a personal experience of God. In this way, a purely abstract approach to knowledge is overcome in favor of that intelligence of the heart which knows how to 'look beyond,' and then is in a position to communicate the mystery of God to the people." While the phrase "intelligence of the heart" is used here in the context of the intellectual formation of the seminarian, one can readily understand how the human formation of the seminarian would be essential to its realization. Furthermore, the concept of the "intelligence of the heart" is integrative, and could very well be used as a hermeneutic for the integration of all four areas of priestly formation.

2. *Pastores Dabo Vobis*, sec. 43: "Of special importance is the capacity to relate to others. This is truly fundamental for a person who is called to be responsible for a community and to be a 'man of communion.' This demands that the priest not be arrogant, or quarrelsome, but affable, hospitable, sincere in his words and heart, prudent and discreet, generous and ready to serve, capable of opening himself to clear and brotherly relationships and of encouraging the same in others, and quick to understand, forgive and console."

3. See *Pastores Dabo Vobis*, sec. 43, to see how the Church understands the "man of communion" as someone who possesses "affective maturity." Furthermore, in sec. 44: "Affective maturity presupposes an awareness that love has a central role in human life." Furthermore, *spiritual affective movements*, feelings which have truths as their object, are located in the heart, which scripture and spiritual theology identify as the spiritual center of the person, even at times equating it with the soul (from IPF Glossary of Terms).

4. Gregory J. Schlesselmann, *The Seminary Rector: Forming Priests in Nazareth* (Omaha, NE: The Institute for Priestly Formation, 2012), 17.

5. See D.V. Hildebrand, *The Heart* (St. Augustine's Press, 2007) for a philosophical argument for the heart as being essential and equal to the intellect and the will.

6. Schlesselmann, 17.

7. *Pastores Dabo Vobis*, sec. 44.

8. J. Cihak, "The Blessed Virgin Mary's Role in the Celibate Priest's Spousal and Paternal Love," Ignatius Insight.com. See also Schlesselmann, *The Seminary Rector*, 54, where Loyal Brother is added as a priestly identity.

9. *Pastores Dabo Vobis*, sec. 21. Pastoral charity is described here as the summation of "spiritual power." Also here the future priest is called to be "freed from all presumption of desire of 'lording over' those in their charge."

10. Ibid., sec. 15. The Holy Spirit "forms and strengthens" the priest with his "pastoral charity" and gives them "an authoritative role in the Church as servants of the proclamation of the Gospel."

11. See *Pastores Dabo Vobis*, sec. 43, for the human qualities of a future priest: "balanced people; strong and free; capable of bearing the weight of pastoral responsibilities. They need to be educated to love the truth; to be loyal; to respect every person; to have a sense of justice; to be true to their word; to be genuinely compassionate; to be men of integrity; and especially, to be balanced in judgment and behavior."

12. *Pastores Dabo Vobis*, sec. 18. "The priest is a man of communion, in his relations with all people he must be a man of mission and dialogue."

13. Ibid., sec. 43. The priest must have the capacity to become a "reader of the depths of human hearts."

14. Ibid., sec. 45. The priest is called to both an "intimate" and "unceasing union with the Trinity." See *Pastores Dabo Vobis*, secs. 12, 16, for the source of the priest's identity is in the Blessed Trinity. See *Pastores Dabo Vobis*, sec. 33, for priestly holiness as understood as "intimacy with God."

15. *Pastores Dabo Vobis*, sec. 26.

16. Ibid., sec. 10.

17. Ibid., sec. 43. The priest must have the affective maturity to be "aware that love has a central role in human life." He must be capable of understanding that "man cannot live without human love" and that "without love his life is meaningless." See *Pastores Dabo Vobis*, 44, where the priest is called to both understand and realize the truth about human love.

18. Blessed John Paul II, *Mulieres Dignitatem* (1988), sec. 31.

19. See Cihak.

20. See Pope Paul VI, *Lumen Gentium* (1964), 21. See also Pope Paul VI, *Presbyterorum Ordinis* (1965), 2. "The office of their ministry (the bishops) has been handed down to a lesser degree indeed, to the priests."

21. *Lumen Gentium*, sec. 26.

22. A *core wound* can be understood as psychological pain, such that an erroneous spiritual structure of belief was formed. Core wounds are fertile grounds for lies that we believe about ourselves, others, and God.

23. *The Spiritual Exercises of St. Ignatius* (Vintage Spiritual Classics, 2000) 118, First Set of Rules for the Discernment of Spirits, rule number 13.

24. *Deliverance* is understood as a private form of exorcism, distinct from the solemn and public liturgical rite, wherein prayer is used to curb the evil spirits in the lives of Christians. Deliverance prayer sets the heart free to worship God first and to free the human heart from the evil spirits that have impeded the call to holiness, so that it may grow in affective maturation and intimacy with Jesus' Sacred Heart (from IPF Glossary of Terms).

25.   See *Pastores Dabo Vobis*, sec. 18. The New Evangelization demands "new fervor; new methods; new expression; priests capable of embodying a new style of pastoral life; profound communion with the pope, bishops, other priests, and the lay faithful."

LEARNING TO BE WITH HIM: FORMING MEN OF COMMUNION THROUGH THREE TASKS IN THE SPIRITUAL LIFE

CHRISTOPHER J. STRAVITSCH

Seminarians must learn to remain with Christ if they are to become men of communion. Learning to remain with Christ was the first responsibility of the disciples whom Jesus called by name: "He appointed twelve...that they might be with him and he might send them forth to preach and to have authority to drive out demons" (Mk 3:14-15). Being "with him" is the essential link that unites the disciples to Jesus and to one another.[1] Called to "live in an intimate and unceasing union with the Father,"[2] an apostle has no mission and bears no authority, except for that which is rooted in and sustained by this communion.

Seminaries are the formative communities for today's disciples and tomorrow's apostles. As such, "the seminary is called to be, in its own way, a continuation in the Church of the apostolic community gathered about Jesus, listening to his word, proceeding towards the Easter experience, awaiting the gift of the Spirit for the mission."[3] During the period of formation, each seminarian must become a person of affective maturity and a man of communion.[4] It is "a time for discernment, a time for learning, a time for vocation…and then, naturally, a time for being with him, a time for praying, for listening to him."[5]

This essay examines how seminaries can form candidates for priesthood into men of communion at the affective and spiritual levels. The topic is approached by making use of Henri Nouwen's three movements in the spiritual life.[6] By learning to identify in seminarians the presence of loneliness, hostility, and illusions, formators can direct seminarians to grow in solitude, hospitality, and prayer. These transitions foster a maturity that is essential for remaining in intimacy with Christ and leading others into the same spiritual communion.

The Movement from Loneliness to Solitude

Society today is breeding lonely men. Broken families, promiscuity and sexual addiction, mass consumerism, the constant distractions of entertainment—these are all signs of an epidemic of loneliness. Relationships are marked by frivolous exchanges, such as an endless stream of text messages. Friendship is defined by connections on social media sites or by the social gatherings that people frequent. Evidently, adults and youth alike are losing the capacity to relate with one another in deep and meaningful ways. Hearts are not engaged nor are young minds stimulated as a result of the painful isolation that is present in so many. Yet, their pain is too great to confront, especially when suffering is understood as an unnecessary weakness. Therefore, many who are lonely convince themselves otherwise and fill their void with distractions.

Recognizing that "the roots of loneliness are very deep,"[7] formators must admit that a number of seminarians still bear traces of their wounds. Formators should remain alert to the signs of loneliness, such as the continuation of the previously noted patterns or any disordered use of goods, which may be an attempt to escape the suffering of loneliness. There are less obvious signs to be aware of, as well. For example, the seminarian who appears to relate well to everyone may actually be relating to no one if his conversations simply consist of sports, rubrics, gossip, and the like, and he rarely speaks from the depths of his heart.

When a formator recognizes a seminarian is lonely, he must help that seminarian face his fears of relating, explore his suffering, and grow in solitude of heart. "To live a spiritual life we must first find the courage to enter into the desert of our loneliness and to change it by gentle and persistent efforts into a garden of solitude."[8] Nouwen posits that the movement from loneliness to solitude marks the beginning of the spiritual life, "because it is the movement from the restless senses to the restful spirit, from the outward-reaching cravings to the inward-reaching search."[9] Truly, it is not so much a movement as it is a calming. If the seminarian has filled his life with noise, then he needs the remedy of restfulness and interior silence.[10] This can lead to discovering a fruitful solitude of the heart. Paradoxically, the formator should encourage the lonely seminarian to spend time alone, instead of filling his life with distractions. He should "take the risk of entering [his] own experience because healing will begin through solidarity with his pain."[11] By understanding his pain and becoming accepting of it, he will open himself to new rivers of grace. The first man, Adam, hid in the Garden of Eden but was found by the Lord God who searched for him; so, too, will the seminarian discover that Christ is searching for him in his loneliness. The *Program of Priestly Formation* describes this process as "moving the candidate from being alone or lonely to entering a holy solitude in communion with God."[12] He learns to be alone with God as he acknowledges and relates his own experience(s) of suffering. As soon as he learns to be interiorly silent and still, then he will begin to receive the love of Christ, who desperately desires to transform his desert of isolation into a garden of solitude, the fertile ground where communion can take root.

Suffering Beneath Loneliness

There are some practical ways a formator can urge the seminarian to spend time exploring the sources and depths of his suffering in solitude. He or she can invite the seminarian to trace the history of his loneliness from childhood to the present. What are his earliest memories of feeling separated from God or others? The formator can ask the seminarian to explore and describe the instances in his life when he may have felt rejected, inferior, abandoned, or hurt by others. The seminarian may benefit from journaling about the story of his pain and loneliness as it unfolds. As he recalls these memories, both the seminarian and formator should pay special attention to four "heavy" emotions: fear, sorrow or hurt, perceived injustice, and anger.[13] Exploring these emotions at length, alongside the life experiences that stir them, will become a path to healing. In a sense, the seminarian aims to befriend his pain by understanding its source and how it has affected him over time. This process frees him to accept his own history, while also empowering him to determine how it will affect him in the present and future.[14] Thus, the seminarian attains the self-possession necessary for affective maturity. At the same time, the formator should remain as a voice of hope and compassion for the seminarian. He cannot completely journey with the seminarian into solitude, since only the seminarian can decide to risk taking this journey into himself. The seminarian will find courage and comfort knowing a trusted formator is remaining nearby, ready to talk and pray each time he reemerges from solitude.

Solitude Grounded in God's Love

A deepening awareness of being loved by God should complement the movement from loneliness to solitude. To accomplish this state of being, spiritual directors, in particular, can offer seminarians some specific points for prayerful meditation. These include the following:

- the reality of being made in the *imago Dei*,[15]
- the efficacious grace of the seminarian's own Baptism[16] and his spiritual adoption as a beloved son of the Father,[17]
- Christ's redemption first offered to him in Baptism and the Holy Spirit dwelling in him as a fruit of that redemption,[18]
- Christ calling him by name to follow after Him as a disciple,[19] and
- Christ sending him on mission as an apostle of Good News.[20]

Meditating on and interiorizing these facets of Christian faith will further form the seminarian's identity in Christ, allowing his solitude to be grounded in the truth of God's love for him. After all, "Solitude is not simply a means to an end…it is the place where Christ remodels us in his own image."[21]

Overall, the movement from loneliness to solitude offers healing from the past and self-possession in the present. It leads to a new receptivity for inner joy and peace at the affective and spiritual levels, and offers a new capacity for becoming a man of communion.[22]

The Movement from Hostility to Hospitality

Seminarians who lack solitude of heart and who have not welcomed the Suffering Servant into their pain are prone to behave in hostile ways that are antithetical to becoming a man of communion. The man of communion exhibits a "peacemaking and nonviolent way of life,"[23] whereas the man of hostility lacks affective maturity and is driven by his feelings.[24] Above all, his hostility is an expression of anger; and anger, as noted above, is usually fueled by experiences of fear, hurt, and injustice. Hostile persons, therefore, act fearful, defensive, aggressive, or suspicious of others. Formators should remain alert for seminarians who often describe feelings of alienation, believe others are a threat, always feel misunderstood, say they are taken for granted, or express paranoia. Hostility is also evidenced in men who overreact about many issues, use sarcasm, or seem to puff up their chest on any number of occasions. Such hostility renders communion impossible and, in fact, facilitates its destruction. When these signs are present in a person, then others are not free to be themselves, and, without authenticity, friendships will not form. Instead, seminarians who are both lonely and hostile become bound together out of fear of each other—fear for themselves. To step out of this circle of pseudo-communion means they might become the next victim of ridicule, so they cling tightly to one another, draw a line in the sand, and cry out "it is us against them!" As formators come to recognize the presence of hostility in a seminarian, they must foster a conversion to hospitality.

In the words of Nouwen, "Hospitality…means primarily the creation of a free space where the stranger can enter and become a friend instead of an enemy."[25] It finds its inspiration in the commandment: "You shall love your neighbor as yourself" (Mk 12:31). Formators can model hospitality by creating a safe and sacred space for seminarians to express themselves freely, to tell their stories, and to be received as they are—in sum, to be welcomed as persons bearing the image of Christ. Seminary teachers can aid in this endeavor, as well, by forming relationships of mutual trust with the students "in which those who teach and those who want to learn can become present to each other, not as opponents but as those who share in the same struggle and search for the same truth."[26] This kind of hospitality disarms hostility and fosters communion. Besides modeling hospitality, there are some practical ways a formator can move a seminarian from hostility to hospitality. These methods include fostering a reconciling spirit, spiritual poverty, reverence, and self-giving charity.

A Reconciling Spirit

Increasing affective maturity in men of communion requires formators to foster "a reconciling spirit in those who aspire to be priests in the spirit of Jesus, who prayed that 'all might be one.'"[27] To that end, teaching forgiveness is another practical help because it eases hostility and creates an environment where enemies can become friends. Unfortunately, several misconceptions about forgiveness, which short circuit the path of healing, are prevalent today. Forgiveness can be mistakenly described as forgetting, excusing, pardoning, or simply accepting offenses. Limited approaches such as these actually inhibit healing and prevent the possibility of genuine reconciliation. When working with a seminarian's hostility, it may be necessary to explore his conception of forgiveness, in order to prevent him from excusing himself from the real work that needs to be done. Enright and Fitzgibbons, leading researchers in this area, define the process of forgiveness in the following way: "People, upon rationally determining that they have been unfairly treated, forgive when they willfully abandon resentment and related responses (to which they have a right), and endeavor to respond to the wrongdoer based on the moral principle of beneficence, which may include compassion, unconditional worth, generosity, and moral love (to which the wrongdoer, by nature of the harmful act or acts, has no right)."[28]

To accomplish forgiveness, the researchers have outlined four phases: uncovering, decision, work, and deepening. The uncovering phase, which comes first, is basically what has been described above in the movement from loneliness to solitude. During the uncovering phase, a person explores how the offense he experienced in his life is negatively affecting him. For example, if a seminarian's hostility toward others is rooted in his wounds from childhood and family life, then he needs to gain insight into these connections. This can be an emotionally painful process, especially if he has only addressed his pain in limited or indirect ways. But if he realizes how much he suffers today from his past, then he can become motivated to change how he deals with the injustices, thus propelling him into the decision phase.

In the decision phase, a person examines how his misconceptions of forgiveness have prevented healing and have led to hostility. The seminarian must open himself up to working toward forgiveness in a new way. Continuing with the previous example, the seminarian with unresolved childhood trauma will decide to begin the process of forgiving his abusive father. When this decision is made, then the work phase follows.

In the work phase, the person tries to understand the offender in his or her context. He develops empathy and compassion toward the offender, learns how to bear with his pain, and eventually aspires to make an act of moral love toward the one who hurt him. So, the seminarian who is working to forgive his abusive father might explore how his father was also a victim of abuse. He will try to empathize with the pain his father has also buried and identify with the pressures that led to the perpetuation of abuse. Gradually beginning to see his father with eyes of compassion will allow the seminarian to respond out of charity. While his father's actions should never be condoned, the seminarian can still choose to offer the gift of forgiveness—an act of moral love that finds its inspiration and source in the mercy of God.

Finally, during the deepening phase, a person continues to draw grace from the experience of forgiveness. He finds meaning in what he has suffered and forgiven. Reflecting on Blessed John Paul II's Apostolic Letter *Salivifici Dolores*[29] can offer inspiration and insight to a seminarian who is searching for meaning in his experience of suffering.

As forgiveness becomes a practice within the lives of seminarians, their hostility will continue to melt away as they open themselves to others with a spirit of hospitality. Overall, formators teaching forgiveness will aid them in fostering a reconciling spirit and forming a community where "all might be one."[30]

Spiritual Poverty

Spiritual directors, in particular, can cultivate hospitality by teaching a spirituality of poverty, for it is by becoming poor that we can become good hosts.[31] In *Poverty of Spirit*, Johannes Baptist Metz writes, "To be able to surrender oneself and become 'poor' is, in biblical theology, to be with God, to find one's hidden nature in God; in short, it is 'heaven.' To stick to oneself and to serve one's own interests is to be damned; it is 'hell.' Here we discover, only too late, that the tabernacle of self is empty and barren."[32]

When a hostile seminarian begins to accept his innate poverty, it frees him from the compulsive need to be liked and loved by others, thereby opening him to greater authenticity in his personal encounters. This poverty becomes a gift to others who can then enter his space with freedom. The good host can say, "'Please enter—my house is your house, my joy is your joy, my sadness is your sadness, and my life is your life, we have nothing to defend, since we have nothing to lose but all to give.'"[33]

Living a spirituality of poverty requires the setting aside of personal agendas, opinions, prejudices, and concerns. Jesus "emptied himself" (Phil 2:7) and so must the candidate for priesthood. He cannot be so full of his own ideas that no space remains for others to express theirs. By realizing he does not have all the answers to the mystery of life, he will gain an "appreciation of the different gifts and charisms, of the diverse vocations and responsibilities which the Spirit offers and entrusts to the members of Christ's Body."[34]

The seminarian will also need to acquire the skill of listening—a skill that seems to be nearly lost in our noisy society. Hospitality requires listening with the conviction that Christ draws near in the presence of others and together we stand on holy ground. Anyone can become a vessel of the Spirit at any given moment, but it is only through listening reverently that we will have "the ears to hear." In this context, learning to be with others in a spirit of hospitality is an essential part of learning "to be with Him." The seminarian's openness will dispose him to be "in communion with the very sentiments and behavior of Christ."[35]

Poverty of spirit is the first of the beatitudes. It is so essential to the Christian life that Metz asserts, "Without it there can be no Christianity and no imitation of Christ."[36] Metz' book can he a helpful resource for a seminarian and his spiritual director. A formator might also make use of the Litany of Humility written by Cardinal Raphael Merry del Val,[37] for the one who "emptied himself" also "humbled himself, becoming obedient to death, even death on a cross" (Phil 2:7, 8).[38]

Reverence

After the seminarian has spent time interiorizing his own identity in Christ through solitude, he can mature by seeking Christ in others.[39] He must learn to see the *imago Dei* in the face of his neighbor, especially those for whom he has hostile feelings. After all, the person of affective maturity cannot be driven by his feelings; instead, his life of feelings should be balanced and integrated with thoughts and Christian values.[40] For example, a seminarian who feels hostility towards others can be challenged to remember that the grace of Baptism is a reality that extends to all his seminarian brothers; they are each tabernacles of the Holy Spirit who is waiting to be discovered and revered. His hostile feelings must be quelled by the gift of reverence. Therefore, formators can teach reverence as part of the movement from hostility to hospitality.

One of the natural dispositions that the Eucharist fosters is reverence—"the yearning to contemplate and bow in adoration before Christ who is really present under the eucharistic species."[41] Therefore, a simple way to teach a seminarian about reverence is to explore his disposition toward the Eucharist and then connect that experience with his relation to others. For example, a formator could ask the seminarian about his gestures of bowing and genuflecting toward Christ in the chapel and discuss the significance of these actions as outward signs of the interior disposition of his heart and the recognition that he is standing on holy ground. Then, the seminarian and the formator can reflect together on how the seminarian could have a similar disposition toward the presence of Christ in others. He can ask himself what gestures convey awe and respect for his neighbor? How might he encounter others in a more sacred way and raise them up in his heart?

The easiest time to cultivate reverence toward others and recognize the presence of Christ in them is during the Communion Rite. The formator should invite the seminarian to quietly reverence Christ's Eucharistic presence in each of the communicants around him. If he struggles with hostility toward a particular seminarian, then he may even be challenged to pray near him in order to contemplate Christ's presence in him during this time. As this way of seeing slowly becomes a habit, the seminarian can also begin reflecting on the presence of the Holy Spirit who remains in them always: "Do you not know that your body is a temple of the holy Spirit within you…" (1 Cor 6:19). Recognizing and reverencing the Spirit in others becomes a way of sharing in the very vision of God. Overall, reverence is a gift possessed by men of communion–now "capable…of receiving the gift of others"[42] they will, in truth, "see God" (Mt 5:8).

A Spirit of Self-Giving Charity

A reconciling spirit offers the seminarian freedom from the past; poverty of spirit then opens him to the blessing of new encounters; and reverence awakens him to the divine gift he receives in the presence of every neighbor. His freedom, poverty, and reverence give him the "real and deep relational capacities" necessary for a man of communion. He enters into "genuine dialogue and friendship," demonstrating "true empathy" and "open[ness] to others."[43] What naturally follows then is "a generosity of spirit" marked by self-giving charity.[44]

Jesus teaches in a parable, "[T]he kingdom of heaven is like a merchant searching for fine pearls. When he finds a pearl of great price, he goes and sells all that he has and buys it" (Mt 13:45-46). Today, seminary formators might say the kingdom of heaven is like a seminarian searching for God. When he finally discovers Christ is in his neighbor, he is set ablaze with self-giving charity toward others. His deep realization that he remains with Christ always–if he only chooses to see Him–fills him with such joy and gratitude that he goes in search of Christ in all. He shares his "pearl of great price" as he generously serves others.

A spirit of pastoral charity expands the seminarian as a man of communion, especially when his service and sacrifice for others becomes spontaneous, rather than confined to the parameters of his pastoral assignment and community responsibilities. Will he go in search of those "who are privileged in God's eyes—the poor, the marginalized, the sick, and the suffering"?[45] Does he show zeal for the works of mercy? Is he willing to serve where needed? "The whole formation imparted to candidates for the priesthood aims at preparing them to enter into communion with the charity of Christ the good shepherd."[46]

The Movement from Illusion to Prayer

Nouwen posits a more basic movement undergirds the other two: the movement from illusion to prayer. Being with God in prayer gives meaning and vitality to the seminarian's solitude and hospitality. "The silence of solitude is nothing but dead silence when it does not make us alert to a new voice sounding from beyond all human chatter. Hospitality leads only to a congested home when nobody is traveling anywhere."[47] It is through the silence of solitude that a seminarian discovers the reality of God's indwelling and receives the truth revealed to him in the person of Christ. It is through hospitality that he becomes totally available to others and learns to journey with them into an encounter with God. A life of prayer integrates the man of communion, who becomes capable of fulfilling the only expectation that the faithful have for priests: "that they be specialists in promoting the encounter between man and God...expert[s] in the spiritual life."[48] Let us, then, explore the illusion of immortality and then prayer.

The Illusion of Immortality

The illusion of immortality[49] is the problem of replacing God with mortal beings, as if they were immortal. This illusion has been seducing mankind since the dawn of creation. Adam and Eve were led into sin as the serpent declared: "You certainly will not die! God knows well that when you eat of it your eyes will be opened and you will be like gods who know good and evil" (Gn 3:4-5). Giving credence to this claim impedes our willingness to approach God as the source of our lives. If prayer is about "being with Him," then this illusion makes that a laughable task. Who needs to remain with God if we can become like gods? Only knowledge of the truth can shatter the illusion: "For there is one God. There is also one mediator between God and the human race, Christ Jesus" (1 Tm 2:5). Prayer facilitates receptivity to this truth, and unceasing prayer is its fruit.

Clearly, no seminarian will consciously subscribe to the belief that his life is his own or that he is immortal, so it will take a perceptive formator to recognize how the illusion of immortality may be masked in the life of a seminarian and how it inhibits him from being completely possessed by God. Formators should look for behaviors whereby a seminarian attributes the qualities of God to others or to himself. In other words, formators should remain alert to patterns of idolatry and fashioning oneself into a god.

Idolatry

"Come, make us a god who will go before us" (Ex 32:1).

This was the cry of the Israelites which led to offering gold and fashioning a molten calf. Their faith was weak without the presence of Moses and, more significantly, without the tangible presence of God. While they may not have intended to worship a false god, but only wanted to symbolize the strength of God with the golden calf, it was not a far jump into idolatry. They wanted an image; they became depraved. The Lord said, "They have quickly turned aside from the way I commanded them, making for themselves a molten calf and bowing down to it, sacrificing to it and crying out, 'These are your gods, Israel...'" (Ex 32:8).

At times, while looking for a role model, seminarians fall into idolatry. A peer, a formator, or a priest they know well might gradually become the object of their adulation. They may not intend to make another person into a god, but through their weakness–insecurity, envy, infatuation, lack of faith, or any number of possibilities–they gradually fall into idolatry. Duped by the illusion of immortality, the seminarian views the other person no longer an *imago Dei*; rather, a boundary is crossed by which the seminarian attributes the qualities of God to the other. Sentimentalism is a clear sign of what is taking place at a deeper level.[50] The seminarian may cling intimately to the mortal one instead of the Savior, placing unrealistic expectations on the idolized person, and incessantly presenting concerns and problems to him. His solitude is terribly at risk as he looks to the other as a source of life instead of remaining "with Him." His hospitality, as well, is no longer life-giving as he aims to please the one he has fashioned into a god.

Formators should also take care not to become the object of a seminarian's sentimentalism. While it may seem flattering

to be so needed and adulated by a directee, the astute formator will want nothing of it and will recognize such adulation
as a symptom of a deeper issue. If suspicions of this grave
illusion arise, whether related to a formator, peer, or someone
else, the formator should ponder the following questions: Is
the seminarian turning to another person more than he turns
to God? After receiving counsel, does he enter into prayerful
solitude or does he rehash the same story with others and
quickly return, looking for more answers? Is his hospitality
rooted in self-giving charity or in the desire to be praised by
someone in particular? Do his actions demonstrate faith in
God or a lack thereof? Exploring these questions with the
seminarian himself may be beneficial, as well. Such reflection may offer piercing clarity of the deeper issue–a lack of
faith and prayer. Idolatry buffers the need to be vulnerable in
prayer; and, since it is rooted in a lie, it will never bear fruit.
The candidate for priesthood will not learn to "remain with
Him" until he is poignantly confronted with his little faith.[51]

Fashioning Oneself as a God

The other side of this illusion is when a seminarian trusts
more in his own abilities than in the power of God. Whether
intentionally or not, he fashions himself into a god. As the
serpent tempted Adam to recreate the world in his own image
and according to his own judgment between good and evil, so
are some seminarians tempted to replace the Savior with their
self. Two ways this may be manifested include self-reliance or
self-righteousness.

Self-reliance. Self-reliance is the more benign side of fashioning oneself into a god. This is the man who relies more on
his own strength than on God's. He lets the weight of every

burden rest on his shoulders and gets involved with numerous charitable works, not knowing how to say "no" when asked for help. As he pulls the harvesting plow on his own, he overextends himself and soon believes the yoke of Christ is heavy rather than light.

This candidate for priesthood must learn to accept his mortality—the innate poverty of humanity[52]—and even to boast in weakness.[53] This can be a genuine challenge for good-intentioned helpers, but a necessary part of maturing into a man of prayer and communion. Human limitations mark the boundary between self-reliance and faith. There is no need to expand the sphere of self by constantly pressing against the limits of our humanity and trying to do the *work* of God without the *help* of God. This is an exhausting endeavor, indeed, which commonly leads to burnout in ministry and eventually, resentment. The self-reliant seminarian must learn to remain with God: "Remain in me, as I remain in you. Just as a branch cannot bear fruit on its own unless it remains on the vine, so neither can you unless you remain in me. . . Whoever remains in me and I in him will bear much fruit, because without me you can do nothing" (Jn 15:4-5).

Accepting the poverty of humanity, on the other hand, allows one to enter the realm of faith by turning to God in prayer, welcoming the gift of grace, and witnessing its fruit. Intimacy with the Triune God is the only lasting sustenance for a life of self-giving charity.

At times, a hint of pride may also fan the flame of self-reliance— for example, when a person in ministry lacks confidence in the talents or dependability of others, finding it safer to bear the burden of responsibilities alone. He becomes guilty of not reverencing the Spirit who is actively at

work in those around him. His intention to lay down his life
is good, but he lacks the humility necessary to invite others
to labor with him in the vineyard of the Lord. Therefore, the
self-reliant man is not a man of communion. Although he
may have some success in preaching the gospel and building
relationships (he may even be well-liked by parishioners!),
his efforts to lead others into communion with God will be
severely retarded by his own lack of communion with God.
He cannot behave as the Messiah and, at the same time,
proclaim His coming. John the Baptist knew this well. By
accepting that he was only a forerunner making straight the
way of the Lord, his joy was made complete. The self-reliant
seminarian will do well by meditating on the words of the
Baptist: "He must increase; I must decrease" (Jn 3:30).[54]

Self-righteousness. When self-reliance is left unchecked and
becomes infested with the sin of pride, it morphs into self-
righteousness. While both can be damaging to oneself and
others, the effects of self-righteousness are felt more dramati-
cally, even, at times, leading to public scandal. The self-righ-
teous seminarian will increasingly act as if the Spirit resides
in him alone while, in fact, each day, he pays less attention to
God's indwelling. His prayer is much like that of the Pharisee
who "took up his position and spoke [a] prayer to himself"
(Lk 18:11). His ego replaces the will of God as he declares
himself to be the savior of the Church, a declaration that
always ends in tragedy. When a mortal man tries to usurp the
Immortal One, his plan of salvation becomes one of violence
instead of love. He is hostile in word and deed, merciless in
judgment, and relentless in forming the Church according to
his own image of good and evil. This candidate for priesthood does not prepare the way of the Lord; rather, he blazes

a path for himself through the Lord's vineyard. Since he does not pray to the Lord, but to himself, he becomes the disciple of his own ideas. He sends himself on a mission to purge the Church of so-called heretics, liturgical abuse, misled parishioners, and so on. He focuses far more on his own judgment of evil than on God. Few are spared as his continence is lived for the kingdom of self, rather than the kingdom of heaven. There is no room for true communion in the kingdom where one reigns apart from God: instead of gathering, it scatters; instead of liberating, it binds; and instead of preaching the freedom of the children of God, it strongholds the letter of the law. In place of love, there is violence.[55] The seminarian's illusion of immortality must be crushed along with the head of the serpent beneath Mary's heel.[56]

In sum, idolatry and fashioning oneself into a god render a life of prayer impossible. When a seminarian falls prey to the illusion of immortality, he does not turn to God as the source of life. Instead, he either prostrates himself at the feet of others or stands alone, trying to force the kingdom of God into existence. His formators will need to unmask the illusion so that he will reach out to God. Idolatry will be remedied as his discipleship is lived at the feet of Jesus, and self-reliance and self-righteousness will be remedied as he discovers himself being sent forth by Him and with Him. For the candidate aspiring to become a man of communion, a life of prayer is indispensable.

Prayer

Prayer is essentially about "being with Him" in intimate and unceasing communion. The candidate for priesthood learns to remain "with the Father through His Son Jesus

Christ in the Holy Spirit."[57] His spiritual life draws him into
the intimacy of the inner life of our Triune God, where he
discovers himself as a subject and recipient of the love of
God. Through prayer, he experiences love, makes it his own,
and participates in it.[58] He cannot live without this love; it is
the air he breathes—the breath of God. This intimacy shared
between God and the seminarian continues in the apostolic
placements inherent in pastoral formation. It is the fruit of
solitude for God. As an apostle, he is sent by Christ and with
Him to build the kingdom of God. Moved by the breath of
God, his spirit of self-giving charity is sustained by grace.
"Solitude and hospitality can bear lasting fruits only when
they are embedded in a broader, deeper, and higher reality
from which they receive their vitality."[59] While much can be
said about the role of prayer in seminary formation,[60] there
are two essential aspects for forming seminarians as men of
communion: prayer as solitude for God and seeking God in
community.

Solitude for God

The practice of solitude is not simply about being alone;
rather, Blessed John Paul II describes "solitude for God" as
being "'alone' before God with God."[61] The art of helping
seminarians enter this "holy solitude in communion with
God" is an essential part of spiritual formation.[62] Silence
fosters an attentive listening to God and an awareness of
God's movement in his life.[63] Only in a context of silence and
solitude will he "first acquire the listening and learning heart
of a disciple."[64] But such a context stands in contrast to the
noise and agitation we are accustomed to in society. Seminary
formators, therefore, are responsible for providing "education

in the deep human meaning and religious value of *silence*, as the spiritual atmosphere vital for perceiving God's presence and for allowing oneself to be won over by it."[65] By integrating external silence into the formation program, the value of silence can be accentuated. This is accomplished by following the prescriptions of regular retreats and days of recollection,[66] but should not be limited to these events. Formators should schedule hours of Eucharistic exposition, encourage personal visits to the Blessed Sacrament in the tabernacle,[67] and provide instruction for *lectio divina* and other methods of meditation.[68] Furthermore, an atmosphere of silence should be integrated with the daily structure of community life.[69] This may include scheduling silent hours in the residence halls or regularly observing silence during some meals. Seminary formators should discuss how well they maintain an atmosphere of external silence and help seminarians appropriate the value of interior silence. The disposition for silence "cultivates a state of diminished interference between a man's heart and the Trinity,"[70] allowing him to be fashioned by grace into the image of Christ.

> The habit of daily prayer and meditation enables seminarians to acquire a personalized sense of how God's salvation has taken hold of their lives and how they might respond to that great grace. This prayer happens in a context of silence and solitude in which they learn to be attuned to God's movements in their lives. It grows and develops into a 'contemplative attitude' that learns to find God in all things. It matures in such a way that it allows for a balanced and unified rhythm of life in action and contemplation, work and prayer, while providing the

future priest with the strength, meaning, and focus he will need in his life.[71]

Every man of communion must make progressive strides in the pursuit of solitude with God if he aspires to be sent on mission as the apostles were and to gather the people into the kingdom of God.

Seeking God in Community

This final stage of growth—seeking God in community—builds upon the others and brings them to completion.

The seminarian who has developed affective maturity by being healed of loneliness and hostility, and who receives the spiritual maturity of being alone with God, will become a priest who is capable of seeking God in communion with others. In fact, at this point, the formation of a faith community gathered around the priest will unfold quite naturally. Through prayerful solitude, the priest's gaze is heavenward; through hospitality, his stance is open to others. The people of God will want to draw near to him because they sense his intimacy with God, witness his inner peace and joy, and they desire it just the same. They recognize the image of Christ recreated in him, so they do not hesitate to approach him, knowing they are welcome in his presence. In fact, they see him going in search of others, desiring to draw them more deeply into intimacy with God, yet, when he finds them, he is filled with such great love it seems as though he has already tasted the intimacy of God in them. This priest who has learned "to be with Him" in unceasing communion is truly His disciple and apostle. Through intimacy with Christ, he now shares in His mission of salvation.[72]

This mature man of communion has no desire to create

a community centered around himself; rather, his joy is made complete as he shares the pearl of great price. By virtue of his continence, he lives for the kingdom of God[73], which already has a foothold in his life. By virtue of his communion with the Church, he continues to gather a community of disciples who will seek God with him and welcome the kingdom into their own lives. He imbues "a spirituality of communion rooted in the mystery of the Triune God and lived out in practical ways in the mystery of ecclesial communion."[74] Indeed, he will be the most natural "teacher of prayer"[75] because he believes what he reads, teaches what he believes, and practices what he teaches.[76] His ministry of the sacraments consummates his communion with God and the people as they seek intimacy with the Lord, stand together gazing heavenward, and wait for His coming.[77]

If priestly formation will journey with candidates for the priesthood along this path of affective and spiritual maturity—toward solitude, hospitality, and prayer—then those candidates will become generous and self-giving priests—men of communion with real and deep relational capacities, who live in intimate and unceasing communion with God, while leading others to do the same.

Appendix

Litany of Humility of Cardinal Raphael Merry del Val

O Jesus! meek and humble of heart,
hear me.

From the desire of being esteemed,
Deliver me, Jesus.
From the desire of being loved,
Deliver me, Jesus.

From the desire of being extolled,
Deliver me, Jesus.
From the desire of being honored,
Deliver me, Jesus.

From the desire of being praised,
Deliver me, Jesus.
From the desire of being preferred to others,
Deliver me, Jesus.

From the desire of being consulted,
Deliver me, Jesus.
From the desire of being approved,
Deliver me, Jesus.

From the fear of being humiliated,
Deliver me, Jesus.
From the fear of being despised,
Deliver me, Jesus.

From the fear of suffering rebukes,
Deliver me, Jesus.
From the fear of being calumniated,
Deliver me, Jesus.

From the fear of being forgotten,
Deliver me, Jesus.
From the fear of being ridiculed,
Deliver me, Jesus.

From the fear of being wronged,
Deliver me, Jesus.
From the fear of being suspected,
Deliver me, Jesus.

That others may be loved more than I,
Jesus, grant me the grace to desire it.
That others may be esteemed more than I,
Jesus, grant me the grace to desire it.

That in the opinion of the world, others
may increase and that I may decrease,
Jesus, grant me the grace to desire it.
That others may be chosen and I set aside,
Jesus, grant me the grace to desire it.

That others may be praised and I unnoticed,
Jesus, grant me the grace to desire it.
That others may be preferred to me in everything,
Jesus, grant me the grace to desire it.

That others may become holier than I,
provided that I become as holy as I should,
Jesus, grant me the grace to desire it.

Our Lady of Humility, pray for us.

NOTES

1. Blessed John Paul II, *Pastores Dabo Vobis* (1992), sec. 60.
2. *Pastores Dabo Vobis*, sec. 45; Pope Paul VI, *Optatam Totius* (1965), sec. 8.
3. *Pastores Dabo Vobis*, sec. 60.
4. United States Conference of Catholic Bishops, *Program of Priestly Formation*, 5th ed. (Washington, DC: USCCB, 2006), sec. 76.
5. Pope Emeritus Benedict XVI, Freiburg, Germany, 26 September 2011, meeting with a group of seminarians at Borromeo Seminary Chapel.
6. The three movements in the spiritual life will be drawn from Henri J.M. Nouwen, "Reaching Out" in *Ministry and Spirituality* (New York: The Continuum Publishing Company, 2002).
7. Nouwen, "Reaching Out," 189.
8. Ibid., 195.
9. Ibid.
10. See James Keating, "Seminary Formation and Interior Silence" in *Nova et Vetera*, English Edition, Vol. 10, No. 2 (2012): 307–19.
11. Nouwen, "Reaching Out," 196.
12. *Program of Priestly Formation*, sec. 110.
13. Most often, anger is an expression of fear, sorrow, or injustice, or combination of these. It is beneficial, then, to explore the emotions beneath one's anger. These provide a language for speaking about and understanding what is happening interiorly at the affective and spiritual levels.
14. Be sure to make use of a trusted counselor if the pain is very deep or if it prohibits docility to formation.
15. Gen 1:27; *Catechism of the Catholic Church*, secs. 355-58, 1701-15.
16. *Catechism of the Catholic Church*, secs. 1262-64.
17. *Pastores Dabo Vobis*, secs. 18-19, 33, 45-46; Gal 4:4-7; Bl. Dom Columba Marmion, *Christ: The Ideal of the Priest* (San Francisco: Ignatius Press, 2005), 276-78, 280-81, 421-22.
18. 1 Cor 6:19; Blessed John Paul II, *Man and Woman He Created Them: A Theology of the Body* (Boston: Pauline Books & Media, 2006), 56:4.
19. Mt 4:18-22; *Pastores Dabo Vobis*, secs. 34-37.
20. Mt 10:1-15, 28:16-30; Jn 20:19-23; Acts 1:8; *Lumen Gentium*, secs. 17, 28; *Pastores Dabo Vobis*, secs. 11-18.
21. Henri J.M. Nouwen, *The Way of the Heart: Desert Spirituality and Contemporary Ministry* (New York: The Seabury Press, 1981), 32.
22. *Program of Priestly Formation*, sec. 76.
23. Ibid., 110.
24. Ibid., 76.

25. Nouwen, "Reaching Out," 221.

26. Ibid., 230.

27. *Program of Priestly Formation*, sec. 110.

28. Robert D. Enright and Richard P. Fitzgibbons, *Helping Clients Forgive: An Empirical Guide for Resolving Anger and Restoring Hope* (Washington, DC: American Psychological Association, 2000), 24.

29. Blessed John Paul II, *Salvifici Dolores* (1984).

30. In addition to the book by Enright and Fitzgibbons cited above, other recommended texts will offer formators insight for helping seminarians with forgiveness, including: Robert D. Enright, *Forgiveness is a Choice: A Step-by-Step Process for Resolving Anger and Restoring Hope* (Washington DC: American Psychological Association, 2001); Michael E. McCullough, Steven J. Sandage and Everett L. Worthington Jr., *To Forgive Is Human: How To Put Your Past in the Past* (Downers Grove, IL: InterVarsity Press, 1997).

31. Nouwen, "Reaching Out," 242.

32. Johannes Baptist Metz, *Poverty of Spirit* (Mahwah: Paulist Press, 1998), 32.

33. Nouwen, "Reaching Out," 242.

34. *Pastores Dabo Vobis*, sec. 59.

35. Ibid., 57.

36. Metz, *Poverty of Spirit*, 21.

37. See the end of this chapter for a copy of Cardinal Raphael Merry del Val's Litany of Humility. For a brief description of the two degrees of humility, the first related to human weakness and the second to the immensity of God's love, see *The Cloud of Unknowing*, chapters 13-15.

38. "Since the disciples must always imitate this love and humility of Christ and bear witness of it, Mother Church rejoices that she has within herself many men and women who pursue more closely the Saviour's self-emptying and show it forth more clearly, by undertaking poverty with the freedom of God's sons, and renouncing their own will" (*Lumen Gentium*, 42).

39. *Pastores Dabo Vobis*, sec. 49.

40. *Program of Priestly Formation*, sec. 76.

41. *Pastores Dabo Vobis*, sec. 48.

42. *Program of Priestly Formation*, sec. 76.

43. Ibid.

44. Ibid.

45. Ibid., 239.

46. *Pastores Dabo Vobis*, sec. 57.

47. Nouwen, "Reaching Out," 249.

48. Pope Emeritus Benedict XVI, Meeting with Priests, Warsaw, May 2006.

49. Nouwen, "Reaching Out," 253.

50. Ibid., 251-53.

51. The calming of the storm at sea will be a helpful Gospel meditation: Mk 4:35-41. See also Ps 62; Is 44:6-23.

52. Metz, *Poverty of Spirit*, 23-28.

53. 2 Cor 12:7-10.

54. Jn 1:19-34, 3:22-30.

55. Nouwen, "Reaching Out," 251-53.

56. Gen 3:15.

57. *Pastores Dabo Vobis*, sec. 45; *Optatam Totius*, sec. 8.

58. *Pastores Dabo Vobis*, sec. 44; Blessed Pope John Paul II, *Redemptor Hominis* (1979), sec. 10.

59. Ibid., 249.

60. *Pastores Dabo Vobis*, secs. 45-50; *Program of Priestly Formation*, sec. 110.

61. Blessed John Paul II, *Man and Woman He Created Them: A Theology of the Body*, 77:1.

62. *Program of Priestly Formation*, sec. 110.

63. St. Ignatius of Loyola's *Rules for the Discernment of Spirits* can be a great aid for teaching seminarians how to be aware, understand, and respond to interior movements. Recommended reading for spiritual directors and directees is Fr. Timothy M. Gallagher, *The Discernment of Spirits: An Ignatian Guide for Everyday Living* (New York: Crossroad Publishing, 2005).

64. *Program of Priestly Formation*, secs. 110, 107.

65. *Pastores Dabo Vobis*, sec. 47.

66. *Program of Priestly Formation*, sec. 110.

67. Ibid., 124.

68. *Pastores Dabo Vobis*, sec. 47; *Program of Priestly Formation*, sec. 123.

69. *Program of Priestly Formation*, sec. 121.

70. Keating, "Seminary Formation and Interior Silence," 309.

71. *Program of Priestly Formation*, sec. 110.

72. Ibid., 42.

73. For an inspiring reflection on continence for the kingdom of heaven see Blessed John Paul II, *Man and Woman He Created Them*, 73:1-85:10.

74. *Program of Priestly Formation*, sec. 108.

75. *Pastores Dabo Vobis*, sec. 47.

76. *Rite of Ordination to the Priesthood*.

77. *Pastores Dabo Vobis*, sec. 48.

How Many Oats Have You Tried to Feed Him?

Ed Hogan

In David Downing's book *Looking for the King* American Tom McCord is having lunch with C.S. Lewis while discussing Arthurian legends. Lewis asks the American about his studies at UCLA.

"[W]hat subjects did you choose for your examinations?" asked Lewis.

"Well," explained Tom, "we don't do things the same way over in the States as you do here. Instead of tutoring and comprehensive exams, we sign up for several classes every semester. Each time you earn a passing grade in a course, you are awarded credits. Then once you've accumulated enough credits, you earn a bachelor's degree."

"Oh yes, that's right", said Lewis, "...I don't think it's a system that would suit me. It sounds like someone judging a horse not by its speed or strength, but by how many oats you've tried to feed it."

Tom grinned at the analogy. "Yes, that's about how it feels from the horse's point of view, too."[1]

Judging a horse not by its speed or strength, but by how many oats you have tried to feed it—that is an interesting analogy, indeed!

I do not intend to suggest that the seminary system is in danger of doing that. At Kenrick-Glennon Seminary, for example, we have a tremendous system for integrating different kinds of feedback on how our seminarians are doing in different dimensions of their formation and for judging their suitability for advancement on those multiple bases and multiple perspectives. I think that, on the whole, we do a good job of judging each seminarian on his "speed and strength" rather than on how many "formational oats" we have tried to feed him. I expect that much the same is true at other places.

At the same time, I wonder if there might be room for improvement in assessing candidates in the area of spiritual formation. Pope Emeritus Benedict XVI said that "The faithful expect only one thing from priests: that they be specialists in promoting the encounter between man and God. The priest is not asked to be an expert in economics, construction or politics. He is expected to be an expert in the spiritual life."[2] As a lay man and a father, I can confirm wholeheartedly what the Holy Father is saying: *this* is what I want from my priests, for myself, and for my children.

But are we doing a good enough job of assessing candidates' "speed and strength"—rather than how many formational oats we have tried to feed them—in *this* area, the area of spiritual formation, the area of promoting the encounter between God and man?

After all, the Program for Priestly Formation says that "spiritual formation is the core that unifies the life of a priest" and that it "stands at the heart of seminary life and is the center around which all other aspects of formation are integrated."[3] Is spiritual formation also the integrating core of our assessment of candidates? And if it is not, could we do a better job of making it so?

We cannot recommend the ordination of a man who is not emotionally healthy, and we have learned the danger of presupposing that he is. We also cannot recommend the ordination of a man who does not have sufficient theological capacity; there are all kinds of ways of assessing that aptitude.

I would contend that we also cannot recommend the ordination of a man who does not have sufficient spiritual maturity, and who does not promote the encounter between God and man. And we cannot "not assess that" on the grounds that we do not know quite *how* to do so. We need to *figure out* how to do so. Parishioners will assess whether a priest promotes the encounter between God and man, and they will vote with their hearts and their feet. We need to go there first.

Can we *quantify* that ability? I have no intention of suggesting that we can or need to do that. But does that mean that we cannot measure it *in any way whatsoever*? I would like to suggest that we *must*, and I would like to start a conversation about ways that we *can*.

Measuring Spiritual Growth

In 2008, Dr. Karen Dwyer and I published a paper in

Seminary Journal. In that paper, we detailed the results of
an investigation into The Institute for Priestly Formation's
10-week summer program for seminarians.[4] As members of
the "Program Review Committee," we wanted to know, and
to be able to report back to the program directors, whether
or not the program was meeting its objectives in a way that
could be measured.

So, we designed a pre-test and post-test self-report measure. The pre-test measure consisted of twenty questions,
each reflecting a general program objective or a specific
course objective, to be answered on a five-point scale. (See
Appendix 1). (In 2008, we switched to a seven-point scale).
The post-test measure consisted of the same twenty questions and five-point scale, plus an additional twenty questions
asking seminarians to rate their growth in that area from the
beginning of the program to the end.

The study—which we have replicated every summer since
2006—has produced interesting and consistent results. Two
findings, in particular, should be mentioned here. These
are: 1) seminarians have consistently reported growth in
the spiritual life, both as measured by statistically significant
differences in their pre-test and post-test scores (using
repeated measures t-tests), and as measured by their "rate
your growth" scores; and 2) in addition, factor analysis of the
"Rate Your Growth" questions has shown the presence of
five distinct factors, all of which load on a single scale, what
we might call a "spirituality" scale.

Dr. Dwyer and I concluded the paper in 2008 by saying:
"This study should challenge those who wonder whether
seminary spiritual formation can produce measurable
changes in thinking and behavior…the results suggest that

a program of spiritual formation can be assessed with measurable objectives."[5]

Lest Dr. Dwyer and I claim too much for this investigation, we must readily admit that the nature of the results was limited by the fact that we used self-reporting measures. But, lest we claim too little, it should be pointed out that this study was only the tip of the iceberg. The story behind the story is that we designed the questions with an eye toward things that could be *observed and assessed in the external forum.*

Can spiritual formation be assessed in the external forum? I think it can, but this line of thinking requires me to say two things by way of follow up.

First, the distinction between "internal forum" and "external forum" is absolutely valid. I want to be clear, from the outset, that I am NOT calling into question the legitimacy of that distinction and its value for the life of the seminarian and priest. This proposal does not require that we violate the internal forum. We are not asking for, or compelling, a manifestation of conscience.

Second, however, the distinction between "internal" and "external" forum may have been overdrawn; and the boundary between the two may need to be re-drawn: *not abolished, but re-drawn.* After all, Jesus' relation with the Father was not simply a matter of the internal forum–thanks be to God! If we re-consider how best to delineate the boundary, it may happen that some things that we previously thought of as belonging strictly and solely to the internal forum will find themselves moving more into the external forum–things like a man's capacity to articulate the life of prayer (which is not the same as the content of his own prayer).

This concept may seem new. Perhaps it is. But, if a man

cannot speak credibly in the external forum about the life of prayer, and, if we cannot confidently say that he promotes the encounter between God and man, then we have to wonder whether he is going to be what the Holy Father says that people expect (and need) from a priest. He may be emotionally healthy–and he needs to be–and we will have assessed that. He may have a solid theological understanding of the faith–and he needs to–and we will have assessed that. But where is this man's spiritual life? Does he promote the encounter between God and man? And have we assessed that?

Because people in the parish will be exposed to a man's emotional health or sickness, part of our job is to assess his state of being to the best of our ability. Because people in a parish will be exposed to a man's theological ability or incompetence, part of our job is to assess it to the best of our ability. If spiritual formation is the core of the life of a priest,[6] and the integrating core of the seminary,[7] then is it not part of our job to assess *that* to the best of our ability, too?

Assessing Spiritual Maturity: Three Strategies

How?

The challenge before us is to come up with some strategy or strategies by which dioceses and seminaries can allow *maturation in the spiritual life* to be reflected in the assessment of candidates for ordination (and even in the growth of priests in ongoing formation). I want to be bold and humble enough to make some proposals–the kind of proposals that will need to be knocked down in order to build something better and truly adequate. Therefore, I propose three possibilities.

From Self-Report to Spiritual Interview

The first possibility is to take the questions from the instrument Dr. Dwyer and I designed to investigate the effectiveness of IPF's ten-week summer program (see Appendix 2), and change the questions from *self-report* measures to *spiritual interview* measures, to be assessed by formation personnel in the external forum.

The advantage of this approach is that it has analogies with other things we already do in the seminary.

For example, theology professors will measure a number of things in an academic assessment. Of course, we will assess whether a student has understood the material–that is simple enough. But we will also assess whether the student is just repeating material from class or has integrated it with his own experience and other studies. Sometimes, with a formal rubric, and sometimes using more informal skill, a professor judges not only the understanding of the material but also the quality and depth of the integration (or lack thereof), and assigns a grade to the student. The assessment *does* involve the judgment of the professor, but that *does not* make it arbitrary or purely subjective. And any professor will tell you that their skill in that kind of assessment grows with instruction, time, and practice. [8]

Likewise, a psychologist measures a number of things in a clinical assessment. She pays attention to eye contact, nervousness, defensiveness, punctuality, dress, and so on. She observes those and many other things, and uses them to make a report about a person. Again, the assessment does involve the judgment of the psychologist, but that does not make it arbitrary or purely subjective. We know that a skillful clinician's report is very helpful in assessing candidates. I think it is fair to say that a person can grow in skillfulness in this area with instruction, time, and effort.

My suggestion is simply that we do something similar along another front–that of spiritual formation. The initial paper with Dr. Dwyer was meant to be a first opening of that front. When you begin to shovel after a deep snowfall, your first paths are not completely clean. It is only when you go back after the first pass that things start to come clear. Similarly, now that we have opened a path by showing what can be done with *self*-reporting measures, the next task is to make the path clear by shifting to *observable* measures.

Does a man know the difference between *thinking about* God and *talking to* God? Can he speak not only about talking to God but also about what it means to become aware of *God's response* to prayer? Does a man speak of the Persons of the Trinity, in particular, or only of "God" in general? Can he name specific relational aspects with regard to each of the Persons of the Trinity? When participating in *lectio divina*, can he name specific words or themes that stand out for him and his reaction to those words or themes, or does he stay on the level of generalities? When speaking of his relationship to the Blessed Mother, can he name feelings and desires in relation to her, or only thoughts about her?

It seems to me that, similar to having an academic or a psychological interview, we could have formation personnel assess certain things in a *spiritual* interview. We could start with the questions from the self-report measure and turn them into interview questions with some basic guidelines or rubrics for "scoring" answers. A man would receive 0 if he could not answer the question; 1, if he answers the question but without giving any specific example; 2, if he answers the question and gives specific examples.[9]

As with academic or clinical assessment, this is not a skill that everyone already has. *But that does not mean it cannot be developed.* As with academic and clinical assessment, one can grow in skillfulness in assessing spiritual formation with instruction, time, and practice.

Practical Exams

When I was a college student, I trained to be an Emergency Medical Technician. After a thorough course of studies, the equivalent of nine credit hours in one semester, I had to take both written and practical exams to be certified. (And that was just for the *basic* certification!)

Many other professions include practical exams at the conclusion of their course of studies. Even CPR training requires a practical exam prior to certification! I wonder if something similar could be developed for seminarians. After all, they are being trained as spiritual physicians.

This assessment could involve the use of case studies. It could involve the use of role-playing. At Kenrick-Glennon seminary, our seminarians do regular "Theological Reflection" sessions, in which they talk about situations that have occurred in their pastoral assignments, and how they responded to those situations. These sessions are part of the external forum. Faculty and staff take part in them, and our observations help to shape the recommendations we make in our assessment of each seminarian.

Such "practical exams" need not be thought of as simply pass/fail exercises. In fact, very few *academic* exams are pass/fail exercises. Most often, the seminary assessment is basically a question of whether a person will get an A or a B. This would be an opportunity to tell a man what we *do* see that calls for commendation, what we *do* see that calls for correction, and what we *do not* see that calls for growth. We are already looking for human, academic, and pastoral issues. There is no need to exclude *spiritual maturity* among the things we are looking for and assessing and giving feedback on in those practical exercises.

Priestly Identities and Observable Behaviors

Pastores Dabo Vobis says that spiritual formation "should be structured according to the meanings and connotations which derive from the identity of the priest and his ministry."[10] Based on a careful reading of *Pastores Dabo Vobis* and Saint Paul, The Institute for Priestly Formation has articulated a series of five such identities. They are: Beloved Son, Chaste Spouse, Spiritual Father, Spiritual Physician, and Good Shepherd. There could be others, but these identities form a genetic (i.e. developmental) sequence that seems to have achieved a measure of stability.

At a 2005 Symposium on Spiritual Formation, Fr. Richard Gabuzda, the Executive Director of The Institute for Priestly Formation, said:

> Methods must be developed to articulate these identities in such a way that a seminarian may be helped to discern the presence or absence of these identities in his own experience as he studies, prays, lives in community, and undertakes an apostolate.... This does not focus on whether or not a candidate can "become" a priest through the fulfilling of various requirements, but on whether or not God has in fact authored this

vocation…maturation in these identities ought to be at the heart of the assessment of the authenticity of a man's call to holy orders.[11]

Following the directive of *Pastores Dabo Vobis* and Fr. Gabuzda's suggestion, I propose that we might take the sequence of identities that IPF has developed and complement that list with *indicators of progression among the identities that can be observed in the external forum.* Again, the process may be likened to the development of the "Deacon Perceiver." And, following the suggestion of one rector, the process might also generate a list of indicators that a man is *not* making progress, similar to Saint Paul's list of the fruits of the flesh and the fruits of the Spirit in Galatians 5:19-23.

Let us invoke the Holy Spirit's help and, borrowing from Fr. Gabuzda's presentation, take a step in that direction, trusting the Spirit to guide us to something more robust than this initial scaffold.

Beloved Son

(Does this man have a basic Christian identity?)

Indicators: Does the man have…

- An ability to talk about the particular and personal love of God for himself?
- Any awareness of God as *Father?*
- A taste of being "Beloved Son" (note that human healing is often needed here)
- A basic confidence in his identity (not grasping for affirmation)

Chaste Spouse

(Is this man being called to live with Jesus as Spouse of the Church?)

Indicators:

- Where are his desires around having a wife and children? Is he aware of any such desires? Has he consciously made a sacrifice of the goodness of having a wife and children, or is he prepared to do so? To what extent have his desires been transformed to spiritual paternity? (Some men come to seminary with little awareness of such desires; some are aware, and are wrestling with the sacrifice; some have committed to the sacrifice and are already well along the path of transformation.)
- Does he speak *joyfully* of the prospect of remaining celibate for the sake of the kingdom? Or is it something he is "willing to do" so that he can become a priest?
- Does he make a gift of himself to others? Is he energized by that?
- Can he speak of his relationship to the Blessed Virgin Mary? Is he aware of her love for him?

Spiritual Father

(Living, with Jesus, His own mission of revealing the Father)

Indicators:

As a spiritual father, this man will have a mission of evangelizing, catechizing, preaching, teaching.

- Is his fatherhood fruitful for others?
- Is his fatherhood life giving for others?
- Does he have the *courage* to say hard things?
- Does he have the *gentleness* to say them with love?

Spiritual Physician

Indicators: Can he…

- Strengthen?
- Nourish?
- Forgive?
- Heal?
- Does he have the ability to distinguish between interior movements? Can he help a person explore the distinction and relation between symptom and cause of sin–i.e., between an action and an interior motivation?

Good Shepherd

(Head and Shepherd)

Indicators: Can he…

- Identify and celebrate the gifts of others (or is he threatened by them)?
- Strategize about how to call forth the gifts of others?
- Identify the weaknesses of others (and love the people in their weakness)?
- Strategize compassionately about how to deal with people's weaknesses?

When all has been said and done, we might only be making explicit and systematic what is already being done implicitly by everyone from bishops to seminary formators (and better by some than others). But the work of making such activities explicit and systematic could be a great service.

Conclusion

Because of its unusual shape, the Saint Louis Arch required some special engineering for its construction. It is fascinating to read about some of the special problems that the engineers faced, and the solutions they came up with, as the arch was being built.

In some ways, I think what we are talking about here is similar: because of the nature of the priesthood, seminary formation faces some special problems, and requires some special "engineering" to support its final goal.

But here is a story worth pondering. At one point, the firm responsible for the actual construction of the arch came to the superintendent of the project and said, "We have a problem. Our engineers tell us that, when we put the last section into place, the whole thing is going to fall down." [12]

The architectural firm believed that the builders were wrong. After some discussion, the superintendent sided with the architects. The project moved forward, and the Arch– which turned out to be structurally sound–has gone on to become world famous.

In some ways, I think we are talking about something similar–minus the fame. There are people who look at the proposal to assess spiritual formation and say, "This can't be done; it's structurally unsound." I think they are wrong. To be sure, there are real challenges. But, instead of saying, "It can't be done," let us face those challenges, and build something that will soar and inspire.

Appendix 1
2007 Pre-Test / Post-Test Questions & Results

Program Survey Questions & Response Choices (5) Always (4) Often (3) Sometimes (2) Seldom (1) Very Seldom	Pre-program Mean	Post-program Mean	Change Score All Sig. <.00	T-test pre-post	Rate Growth Mean (5) Great (4) Moderate (3) Some (2) Little (1) None
1. I am able to pray with my heart's desires.	3.36	4.04	.69	8.90	4.38
2. Praying with my heart's desires leads me into experiencing the loving presence of Jesus.	3.39	4.08	.69	7.24	4.19
3. Praying with my heart's desires draws me toward experiencing the loving presence of the Blessed Virgin Mary.	2.75	3.54	.79	6.60	3.70
4. I have an interior understanding of how to see the Trinity's love for me in prayer.	2.68	3.86	1.17	12.10	4.05
5. I experience how Trinitarian prayer leads to my personal growth in holiness.	2.88	3.90	1.02	9.59	4.09
6. I am experiencing and understanding how to integrate prayer with my daily life.	3.40	4.21	.82	9.13	4.21
7. I am experiencing and understanding how to consistently integrate prayer with my studies.	2.98	3.61	.61	5.63	3.63

Program Survey Questions & Response Choices (5) Always (4) Often (3) Sometimes (2) Seldom (1) Very Seldom	Pre-program Mean	Post-program Mean	Change Score All Sig. <.00	T-test pre-post	Rate Growth Mean (5) Great (4) Moderate (3) Some (2) Little (1) None
8. I am experiencing and understanding how a healthy integration of celibate chastity occurs in everyday faith.	3.26	4.03	.77	7.29	4.06
9. I understand the difference between reading Scripture and praying with Scripture.	3.59	4.47	.87	7.58	3.84
10. When I pray with the Scriptures, I notice that I am drawn to a particular word or phrase.	3.43	4.03	.60	5.25	3.77
11. When I pray with the Scriptures and notice that I am drawn to a particular word or phrase, I also notice my interior response to that word or phrase.	4.21	3.71	-.49	5.84	3.75
12. I am experiencing and understanding what it means to exercise the gift of spiritual discernment.	4.21	3.80	-.41	3.54	4.11
13. I am experiencing and understanding how to integrate the gift of spiritual discernment with my pastoral service.	2.97	3.70	.73	6.77	3.88
14. I am aware of the presence of Christ in my apostolic service.	3.50	4.08	.49	6.03	3.99

Program Survey Questions & Response Choices (5) Always (4) Often (3) Sometimes (2) Seldom (1) Very Seldom	Pre-program Mean	Post-program Mean	Change Score All Sig. <.00	T-test pre-post	Rate Growth Mean (5) Great (4) Moderate (3) Some (2) Little (1) None
15. Reflecting on the presence of Christ in my apostolic service enriches my prayer life.	3.49	4.01	.51	4.38	3.95
16. My experience in apostolic service contributes to my spiritual growth.	3.62	4.08	.46	4.61	3.94
17. My prayer fosters a faith that promotes justice and mercy in our world.	3.51	3.97	.47	4.73	3.60
18. I understand the unique identity and spirituality of the diocesan priesthood.	3.22	4.18	.96	9.30	4.38
19. I am experiencing how prayer enhances a genuine fraternity with my fellow seminarians.	3.23	4.07	.84	7.39	3.81
20. I am experiencing how prayer enhances friendships.	3.50	4.12	.61	4.13	3.86

Appendix 2
The Institute for Priestly Formation Summer 2008 Post-Program Survey

Please take a minute to complete this evaluation. Your comments will assist us in determining the overall effectiveness of this program. (Your ID will be used to match your post test for statistical analysis purposes only; summer program assessment will be analyzed off-campus, and your identity will be not be revealed to anyone.) **Please circle the number that best corresponds with your answer.**

1. I am able to distinguish between my thoughts, feelings, and desires.

7-Always 6-Usually 5-Often 4-Occasionally 3-Often Not 2-Rarely 1-Never

*   From the beginning of the program until now, I would rate my growth in this area as:

7-Very Great 6-Great 5-Moderate 4-Some 3-Little 2-Very Little 1-None

2. I am able to pray with my heart's desires.

7-Always 6-Usually 5-Often 4-Occasionally 3-Often Not 2-Rarely 1-Never

*   From the beginning of the program until now, I would rate my growth in this area as

7-Very Great 6-Great 5-Moderate 4-Some 3-Little 2-Very Little 1-None

3. Praying with my heart's desires leads me into experiencing the loving presence of Jesus.

7-Always 6-Usually 5-Often 4-Occasionally 3-Often Not 2-Rarely 1-Never

*   From the beginning of the program until now, I would rate my growth in this area as:

7-Very Great 6-Great 5-Moderate 4-Some 3-Little 2-Very Little 1-None

4. Praying with my heart's desires draws me toward experiencing the loving presence of the Blessed Virgin Mary.

7-Always   6-Usually   5-Often   4-Occasionally   3-Often Not   2-Rarely   1-Never

* From the beginning of the program until now, I would rate my growth in this area as:

7-Very Great   6-Great   5-Moderate   4-Some   3-Little   2-Very Little   1-None

5. I practice the silence and solitude necessary for contemplative prayer.

7-Always   6-Usually   5-Often   4-Occasionally   3-Often Not   2-Rarely   1-Never

* From the beginning of the program until now, I would rate my growth in this area as:

7-Very Great   6-Great   5-Moderate   4-Some   3-Little   2-Very Little   1-None

6. I have an interior understanding of how to see the Trinity's love for me in prayer.

7-Always   6-Usually   5-Often   4-Occasionally   3-Often Not   2-Rarely   1-Never

* From the beginning of the program until now, I would rate my growth in this area as:

7-Very Great   6-Great   5-Moderate   4-Some   3-Little   2-Very Little   1-None

7. I experience how Trinitarian prayer leads to my personal growth in holiness.

7-Always   6-Usually   5-Often   4-Occasionally   3-Often Not   2-Rarely   1-Never

* From the beginning of the program until now, I would rate my growth in this area as:

7-Very Great   6-Great   5-Moderate   4-Some   3-Little   2-Very Little   1-None

8. I am experiencing and understanding how to integrate prayer with my daily life.

7-Always 6-Usually 5-Often 4-Occasionally 3-Often Not 2-Rarely 1-Never

*   From the beginning of the program until now, I would rate my growth in this area as:

7-Very Great 6-Great 5-Moderate 4-Some 3-Little 2-Very Little 1-None

9. I am experiencing and understanding how to consistently integrate prayer with my studies.

7-Always 6-Usually 5-Often 4-Occasionally 3-Often Not 2-Rarely 1-Never

*   From the beginning of the program until now, I would rate my growth in this area as:

7-Very Great 6-Great 5-Moderate 4-Some 3-Little 2-Very Little 1-None

10. I am able to integrate the dynamics of prayer with liturgical celebrations.

7-Always 6-Usually 5-Often 4-Occasionally 3-Often Not 2-Rarely 1-Never

*   From the beginning of the program until now, I would rate my growth in this area as:

7-Very Great 6-Great 5-Moderate 4-Some 3-Little 2-Very Little 1-None

11. I am able to acknowledge sexual feelings and desires.

7-Always 6-Usually 5-Often 4-Occasionally 3-Often Not 2-Rarely 1-Never

*   From the beginning of the program until now, I would rate my growth in this area as

7-Very Great 6-Great 5-Moderate 4-Some 3-Little 2-Very Little 1-None

12. When I acknowledge sexual feelings and desires, I am able to relate them to God in prayer.

7-Always 6-Usually 5-Often 4-Occasionally 3-Often Not 2-Rarely 1-Never

* From the beginning of the program until now, I would rate my growth in this area as:

7-Very Great 6-Great 5-Moderate 4-Some 3-Little 2-Very Little 1-None

13. When I relate my sexual feelings and desires to God in prayer, I am able to receive the love of the Trinity.

7-Always 6-Usually 5-Often 4-Occasionally 3-Often Not 2-Rarely 1-Never

* From the beginning of the program until now, I would rate my growth in this area as:

7-Very Great 6-Great 5-Moderate 4-Some 3-Little 2-Very Little 1-None

14. I am experiencing and understanding how a healthy integration of celibate chastity occurs in everyday faith.

7-Always 6-Usually 5-Often 4-Occasionally 3-Often Not 2-Rarely 1-Never

* From the beginning of the program until now, I would rate my growth in this area as

7-Very Great 6-Great 5-Moderate 4-Some 3-Little 2-Very Little 1-None

15. I understand the difference between reading Scripture and praying with Scripture.

7-Always 6-Usually 5-Often 4-Occasionally 3-Often Not 2-Rarely 1-Never

* From the beginning of the program until now, I would rate my growth in this area as:

7-Very Great 6-Great 5-Moderate 4-Some 3-Little 2-Very Little 1-None

16. When I pray with the Scriptures, I notice that I am drawn to a particular word or phrase.

7-Always 6-Usually 5-Often 4-Occasionally 3-Often Not 2-Rarely 1-Never

* From the beginning of the program until now, I would rate my growth in this area as:

7-Very Great   6-Great   5-Moderate   4-Some   3-Little   2-Very Little   1-None

17. When I pray with the Scriptures and notice that I am drawn to a particular word or phrase, I also notice my interior response to that word or phrase.

7-Always   6-Usually   5-Often   4-Occasionally   3-Often Not   2-Rarely   1-Never

* From the beginning of the program until now, I would rate my growth in this area as

7-Very Great   6-Great   5-Moderate   4-Some   3-Little   2-Very Little   1-None

18. I am experiencing and understanding what it means to exercise the gift of spiritual discernment.

7-Always   6-Usually   5-Often   4-Occasionally   3-Often Not   2-Rarely   1-Never

* From the beginning of the program until now, I would rate my growth in this area as

7-Very Great   6-Great   5-Moderate   4-Some   3-Little   2-Very Little   1-None

19. I am experiencing and understanding how to integrate the gift of spiritual discernment with my pastoral service.

7-Always   6-Usually   5-Often   4-Occasionally   3-Often Not   2-Rarely   1-Never

* From the beginning of the program until now, I would rate my growth in this area as:

7-Very Great   6-Great   5-Moderate   4-Some   3-Little   2-Very Little   1-None

20. My experience in apostolic service contributes to my spiritual growth.

7-Always   6-Usually   5-Often   4-Occasionally   3-Often Not   2-Rarely   1-Never

*   From the beginning of the program until now, I would rate my growth in this area as

7-Very Great   6-Great   5-Moderate   4-Some   3-Little   2-Very Little   1-None

21. I am aware of the presence of Christ in my apostolic service.

7-Always   6-Usually   5-Often   4-Occasionally   3-Often Not   2-Rarely   1-Never

*   From the beginning of the program until now, I would rate my growth in this area as:

7-Very Great   6-Great   5-Moderate   4-Some   3-Little   2-Very Little   1-None

22. Reflecting on the presence of Christ in my apostolic service enriches my prayer life.

7-Always   6-Usually   5-Often   4-Occasionally   3-Often Not   2-Rarely   1-Never

*   From the beginning of the program until now, I would rate my growth in this area as:

7-Very Great   6-Great   5-Moderate   4-Some   3-Little   2-Very Little   1-None

23. My prayer fosters a faith that promotes justice and mercy in our world.

7-Always   6-Usually   5-Often   4-Occasionally   3-Often Not   2-Rarely   1-Never

*   From the beginning of the program until now, I would rate my growth in this area as:

7-Very Great   6-Great   5-Moderate   4-Some   3-Little   2-Very Little   1-None

24. I understand the unique identity and spirituality of the diocesan priesthood.

7-Always   6-Usually   5-Often   4-Occasionally   3-Often Not   2-Rarely   1-Never

*   From the beginning of the program until now, I would rate my growth in this area as:

7-Very Great   6-Great   5-Moderate   4-Some   3-Little   2-Very Little   1-None

25. When I hear stories about the daily life of a diocesan priest, my heart is enlivened.

7-Always 6-Usually 5-Often 4-Occasionally 3-Often Not 2-Rarely 1-Never

*   From the beginning of the program until now, I would rate my growth in this area as:

7-Very Great   6-Great   5-Moderate   4-Some   3-Little   2-Very Little   1-None

26. I am experiencing how prayer enhances a genuine fraternity with my fellow seminarians.

7-Always 6-Usually 5-Often 4-Occasionally 3-Often Not 2-Rarely 1-Never

*   From the beginning of the program until now, I would rate my growth in this area as:

7-Very Great   6-Great   5-Moderate   4-Some   3-Little   2-Very Little   1-None

27. I am experiencing how prayer enhances friendships.

7-Always 6-Usually 5-Often 4-Occasionally 3-Often Not 2-Rarely 1-Never

*   From the beginning of the program until now, I would rate my growth in this area as:

7-Very Great   6-Great   5-Moderate   4-Some   3-Little   2-Very Little   1-None

28. I would rate my spiritual growth over the course of the summer program as:

7-Very Great   6-Great   5-Moderate   4-Some   3-Little   2-Very Little   1-None

Open-ended Questions

29. What was most helpful for your spiritual growth in this ten-week program?

30. Was there anything that was not helpful to your spiritual growth or that was detrimental to it in this program?

31. How was your apostolic service helpful to your spiritual growth?

32. If you could change anything in this program, what would it be; and how could it be changed?

33. Please add any additional comments.

Thank you!

NOTES

1. David C. Downing, *Looking for the King.* (San Francisco: Ignatius Press, 2010), 30-31.
2. Pope Emeritus Benedict XVI, *Address by the Holy Father Meeting the Clergy*, Warsaw Cathedral, May 25, 2006.
3. United States Conference of Catholic Bishops (USCCB), *Program of Priestly Formation*, 5th ed. (Washington DC: USCCB, 2006), sec. 115. The Holy Father's point about what the faithful expect from priests explains why the *PPF* puts that emphasis on spiritual formation: because the goal is to form a priest who is an expert at promoting the encounter between man and God.
4. Karen Dwyer, "Assessment of the Summer Program of Spiritual Formation for Diocesan Seminarians: Pre- and Post-Self-Report Measures Indicate Significant Change." *Seminary Journal* 14 no:3 (2008): 37-41.
5. Karen Dwyer and Edward Hogan, "Assessment of Spiritual Formation for Diocesan Seminarians." Seminary Journal (Winter 2008, 37-41).
6. Blessed John Paul II, *Pastores Dabo Vobis* (1992), sec. 45.
7. USCCB, *Program of Priestly Formation*, sec. 115.
8. This essentially coincides with the line of reasoning articulated by Bernard Lonergan in his oft-repeated insistence that "objectivity is the fruit of authentic subjectivity." For the initial articulation of this idea, see Bernard Lonergan, S.J., *Insight: A Study of Human Understanding*, University of Toronto Press, Scholarly Publishing Division, 5th ed., (April 6, 1992), chapter 13. For the development of the idea, see Bernard Lonergan, S.J., *Topics in Education: The Cincinnati Lectures of 1959 on the Philosophy of Education*, University of Toronto Press, Scholarly Publishing Division, 1 ed. (July 1, 1988), pp. 175-6 and Bernard Lonergan, S.J., *Philosophical and Theological Papers, 1965-1980*, University of Toronto Press, Scholarly Publishing Division, 2nd rev. ed., (June 1, 2004), pp. 202, 204, 339, 389-90. For the mature deployment of the idea, see Bernard Lonergan, S. J., *Method in Theology*, University of Toronto Press, Scholarly Publishing Division, 2nd ed. (June 1, 1990), pp. 238, 265, 292, 338.
9. Again, the examples need not come from the seminarian's own prayer life. In his book, *The Discernment of Spirits*, Fr. Tim Gallagher draws beautiful examples of how the Rules for the Discernment of Spirits work from the lives of Saints, historical figures, and contemporary people.
10. *Pastores Dabo Vobis*, sec. 45.
11. Fr. Richard Gabuzda, "Relationship, Identity, Mission: A Proposal for Spiritual Formation," in *Interiority for Mission: Spiritual Formation for Priests of the New Evangelization.* (Fourth Annual Symposium on the Spirituality and Identity of the Diocesan Priest. Held at St. John Vianney

Theological Seminary, March 3-6, 2005.), 46-47.

12. George B. Hartzog, Jr., "Will the Arch Stand?" in *The Gateway Arch: An Architectural Dream* (Jefferson National Parks Association, 2010), 72-73.

CPSIA information can be obtained at www.ICGtesting.com
Printed in the USA
BVOW08s2259201113

336798BV00002B/2/P